# Cut Flowers, Foliage & Fruits of the Southeast

# Cut Flowers, Foliage & Fruits of the Southeast

## Four Seasons of Floral Design

LEE HEMMINGS CARLTON

Globe
Pequot

Essex, Connecticut

# Globe
# Pequot

An imprint of The Rowman & Littlefield Publishing Group, Inc.
4501 Forbes Blvd., Ste. 200
Lanham, MD 20706
www.rowman.com

Distributed by NATIONAL BOOK NETWORK

British Library Cataloguing in Publication Information available

Library of Congress Cataloging-in-Publication Data available

ISBN 978-1-4930-4442-9 (cloth : alk. paper)
ISBN 978-1-4930-4443-6 (electronic)

∞™ The paper used in this publication meets the minimum requirements of American National Standard for Information Sciences—Permanence of Paper for Printed Library Materials, ANSI/NISO Z39.48-1992

*For my parents,*

*Anna Cruikshank Carlton*

*and*

*John Morrison Carlton Jr.*

# CONTENTS

# ACKNOWLEDGMENTS

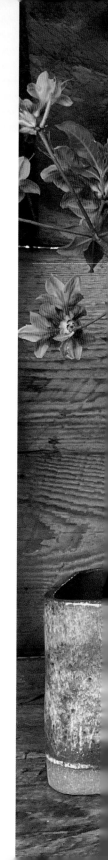

I would first like to thank my dear friend Kelly Perry. When the idea of doing a book about native cut flowers popped into my head, I called her almost immediately, and not only did she listen patiently as I breathlessly described what I wanted to do, she also got me to sit down with her long enough to hash out how best to approach the project. Serendipity took over not long after that when Globe Pequot editor Katie O'Dell reached out to Kelly about doing a similarly themed book. The day I delivered a big load of both native and field-grown stems for one of Kelly's Boone, North Carolina, flower workshops, she put a Globe Pequot book in my hand and told me she had found a publisher for me.

Thanks to Katie O'Dell for seeking Kelly out, helping me get my vision organized, and, through sweet persistence, nudging me further in the right direction with my photos. Thanks to Amy Lyons for taking the editorial reigns after Katie was transferred to Falcon Guides. She guided me to the finish line in the midst of a global pandemic.

A big shout out goes to Bachman Smith IV, my friend the former English teacher, now attorney, for reading through and offering up both ideas and needed commentary at various stages of the project. His enthusiasm and support were integral in me getting the writing work I needed to do completed properly and more eloquently.

Also, Sydney Farris—for lending a keen eye and capable hands with the camera when I was unable to be both in front of and behind the lens.

Last but not least, my husband, artist David Wimmer, for the long conversations about color, for the laughter when I get too serious, for building the structures that I make flowery messes in, and, most of all, for never holding me back.

# INTRODUCTION

I'VE SPENT A LIFETIME CUTTING, testing, and designing with native plants from all over the Southeast. There are quite a few good reasons to appreciate and cultivate native plants. They are naturally the centerpiece of the region, so why shouldn't they be the centerpiece of your dining table? From the mountains of Southern Appalachia, into the Piedmont Plateau, and all the way down to the Atlantic and Gulf Coastal Plains, the native plants of the southeastern United States provide an abundance of cut flowers, foliage, fruit, and berries that add regional character to any bouquet, vase, or wreath throughout the year.

So many wonderful choices exist in plentitude within easy and free reach. They fill ditches, climb trees, descend slopes, and populate the roadside, just waiting for someone to come along and appreciate them enough to bring them home. Many of the common names end with "weed." Ralph Waldo Emerson wrote, "What is a weed? A plant whose virtues have yet to be discovered." I see and embrace those virtues every time I find a delightful new bloom, leaf, or berry that either makes it for a week in a vase or ages gracefully in a wreath.

Although regions of the Southeast differ in climate and topography, they are botanically related. Mountain laurel, for example, has followed creeks and rivers from the Appalachian Mountains east to coastal Virginia, south to the Florida Panhandle, and west to Mississippi. Over time, some natives have evolved into different species in response to their growing environment or isolation, while others remain the same throughout their distribution.

In this manual I provide descriptions of over eighty native plants of all types that are great for floral design, including harvest and postharvest tips to maximize their vase life. Through the step-by-step design series, I will show you how they can be used each season—either alone or with locally grown or foraged non-native species. I took almost every single photo and created every design series in this book. The goal: to put a microscope on the beautiful world of plants just outside your door, and to inspire you to find uses for them in hopes that it will further recognition and cultivation of truly native species of the Southeast. The book is small enough to carry in your car as a field guide and pretty enough to leave on your coffee table when you aren't referencing it. In a world of increasing homogeneity, we need these natives, and they need us!

# OVERVIEW

## The Southeast Then and Now and Why It Matters

The Columbian era began in 1492, and the sudden arrival of humans from another continent initiated a cataclysmic change, introducing, by intention or accident, foreign fungus, plants, and insects that continue to alter our landscape—sometimes drastically—to this day.

Consider the majestic chestnut forests of Appalachia: A fungus from Asia completely obliterated them in the span of just fifty years. If I could travel back in time, my number one destination would be that forever-gone forest. I would give anything to walk among trees that were giant enough to dwarf an entire family standing at the base of just one. I can now only imagine the sound of the wind through their branches and the high, open shade that their canopy created. I have ridden by horseback through areas that were once their domain, and their stumps continue to persevere like ghosts, reminding me just how precious trees are and how quickly they can disappear with the unfortunate introduction of something as tiny as a fungal spore or insect.

In recent years the evergreen hemlock, another distinguished species of the Appalachian forest, has been nearly leveled by a tiny insect called the woolly adelgid. Native to North America but lacking a natural predator in numbers enough to control it, this bug's population exploded under a perfect storm of conditions and turned entire mountainsides that were covered in the deep green of hemlock needles into skeletons, standing bleached and sad until winter winds popped their tops off and tossed them down like broken toothpicks into the dense blanket of rhododendron below.

The majority of the Piedmont Plateau—our most populated region of the Southeast—is hardly recognizable as the same place that was once blanketed by a diverse array of both giant hardwood and evergreen species, including stands of longleaf pine.

The mighty longleaf forests of the coastal plain suffered a different fate. Stretching across the coastal plain from Virginia all the way into eastern Texas, the longleaf forest once covered an astounding ninety million acres of coastal plain. The giant pines—towering 150 feet over a vast prairie understory with nearly four hundred species per cubic yard—that evolved to thrive with frequent wildfires have been reduced to a mere 5 percent of their former range as a result of extensive clear-cutting for the valuable lumber. The stands that remain, thanks to private and government conservation and management efforts, are islands of diversity floating in a sea, surrounded by either soilless wasteland rendered useless from the erosion that clear-cutting causes; modern agriculture, which levels everything from the ponds used for irrigation to the roadside ditches where the irrigation pivot ends; or the never-ending march of suburbanization, with its endless miles of chain stores and planned communities filled with things made on the other side of the world that weren't meant to last.

After all that carnage, what are we left with? Quite a lot, actually. From the stately magnolia trees to the ubiquitous yet truly gorgeous pokeweed, this region is gifted with an astounding array of fabulous plants that perform beautifully as cut stems in floral design. The forest giants may now only exist in our imaginations and a few rare pockets of protected land, but many of the less commercially valuable species have proliferated in the wake of their demise. If you peer into the soul of a single plant, you will glimpse not only their inherent beauty but also their story of survival through adaptation that goes back countless generations.

I was fortunate enough to grow up underneath the longleaf forest on a large tract handed down from one generation to the next and now carefully managed under a conservation easement. That easement ensures that the next generations will have the same opportunity to hear the slightest breeze catch the needles towering above and see the blooming wiregrass move in waves below. I've followed endangered gopher tortoises to their sandy dens and watched them pull in their feet and slide like magic down into those cool dark holes they call home. I've waded with my father through the bogs filled with several species of alien-looking carnivorous plants, and in October witnessed again and again the rainbow of tiny flowers floating on their long thin stems like confetti over the wiregrass. I now live above and hike deeper into a part of the Appalachian forest above the Elk River and a gorge they call Nowhere, and while being dive-bombed by countless hummingbirds have seen stands of lilies towering over my head by the hundreds, like candelabra in a cathedral with a Carolina blue sky serving as the ceiling that never ends. I can tell you that these ancient theaters possess precious beauty like no other and are worth saving, even if it is only one flower at a time.

## What Is a Native Plant?

Native plants are flora that are endemic to a particular geographic region. They have evolved over time in response to differing geologic and climatic conditions and as a group—along with the native fauna—characterize specific ecosystems. I consider native plants of the Southeast to be species that were here before the arrival of Europeans. Native plants of this area have been growing and adapting along with their native pollinators over thousands of years. Their distribution may or may not have been affected by the presence of Native Americans.

## Scientific Names, Cultivars, and Nativars

The scientific name of a plant is Latin based and made up of two words—the genus and the species—put together, with the genus name capitalized. For example, what is known commonly as flame honeysuckle has the Latin name *Lonicera sempervirens*.

### CULTIVARS
When a particular plant—either wild or bred—is singled out for particular positive attributes and propagated by either planting its seeds or through vegetative means (rooted cuttings, division, or tissue culture), it is also given a cultivar name that is capitalized in single quote marks following the species name. For example, *Monarda didyma* 'Raspberry Wine' is a strain of bee balm that displays raspberry-pink flowers rather than the typical red ones of the species.

This strain has also shown itself to be less prone to getting powdery mildew on its foliage than the straight species. Both of those positive attributes made that particular strain an ideal candidate to be singled out, propagated, and distributed as a garden or landscape plant.

## NATIVARS

A newer term, "nativar," has been coined to describe a plant that, although its parentage consists of one or more native species, has been intentionally bred and selected for particular attributes that differ from the straight species of the parents. Ornamental qualities that may be selected include differences in flower size, foliage or flower color, growth habit, seed set, disease resistance, and even ease of propagation. Nativars are multiplied by rooting cuttings of the parent plant or by tissue culture. That means every single plant out there of that variety has the same exact DNA—they are clones. Unlike open pollinated progeny, they are not able to constantly evolve and reselect themselves to best suit the ever changing environment they exist within.

There has been some research into whether native pollinators visit locally endemic straight species more than nativars, and, quite frankly, even though the box store tag may boast that the plant is a US native, it will only bring a fraction of life-giving nectar to local insects.

## INTRODUCED OR NATURALIZED SPECIES

Many plants that were introduced to the New World from another continent either intentionally or by accident have escaped cultivation and naturalized in areas that accommodate their growing needs. These opportunistic species include dandelion, chicory, Queen Anne's lace, oxeye daisy, mullein, and all but one *Mentha* (mint) species. These may be medicine to some and a bane to others. For example, although some consider Queen Anne's lace a pesky garden weed, I love adding the flowers that I find along roadsides to arrangements, and I even cultivate a most enchanting dark-flowered strain. Conversely, chicory is an obnoxious pest when it populates our farm's pastures and fields, and is difficult to manage due to its telephone-pole-like taproot. Many folks, however, enjoy its sky-blue flowers, and quintessential New Orleans coffee is flavored with its roasted root, which evolved out of necessity when imported coffee was in short supply.

## INVASIVE NON-NATIVE SPECIES AND THEIR IMPACT ON THE ECOSYSTEM

Native plants do not include species that have been introduced either intentionally or accidentally by settlers from another continent within the last five hundred years. Some introduced species have become terribly invasive and have had a catastrophic effect on our landscape. Kudzu, for example, "the vine that ate the south," is a perennial vine in the legume family originally from an area in Japan where winters get cold enough to keep its growth in check. It was planted in the Southeast, where winters are typically mild, beginning in 1883, next to porches, bringing cool, shady relief in our sweltering summers; on banks, roadsides, and fields to prevent erosion; and in fields as a cover crop that could provide high-protein fodder for cattle. Little did we know then of its destructive potential, or that this green monster would quickly gobble up trees, shrubs, power lines, buildings, and cars and smother native species and anything, really, that isn't moving. Its infestation has created an alien landscape out of 7.4 million acres and counting.

Other non-native plant "thugs," which may now seem part of the fabric that weaves our southern landscape together, have had a negative impact on our

*Multiflora rose hips, Asiatic bittersweet, and Japanese privet berries—pretty invasive!*

native plant communities. The list is long, so I'll mention just a few, knowing you are likely familiar with some of the worst because, yes, they are pretty.

## Why Use Native Plants in Floral Design?

Native plants are an ideal choice for use in floral design for many reasons. The more we recognize, use, share, and cultivate natives for floral work, the better chance they have of surviving a future filled with the constant onslaught of overly bred clones that big industry favors. Natives are beneficial from an ecological standpoint because they maintain biodiversity, host native pollinators, slow soil erosion, and have a built-in resistance to wild swings in weather. They require fewer nutrients and less water than introductions that were pumped full of who knows what to make them visually appealing enough for you to bring them home from the garden center. Durability is one of their calling cards, although it may take patience to realize it.

Aesthetically speaking, native plants are perfect additions or even centerpieces in floral design because they provide regional character—a sense of place—in a growingly homogenized world. Native cut flowers, foliage, and berries are not grown on another continent to then hop on a plane and arrive in your hands a week later filled with preservatives to maintain their fresh look. They are fresh, locally abundant, and present for your enjoyment. They will continue to be there if you follow the rules of foraging that I lay out. They have an even better chance if you choose to encourage them in your garden or use them to border your field.

## Seasonal Expectations

The internal clocks of natives have evolved to be more attuned to their local seasonality and fluctuation of weather than non-natives. Introduced plants often break dormancy before spring has truly arrived, while natives take their time to wake up. Natives seem to know better than to jump the gun after a warm spell in late winter. This can be observed across the Southeast—take a drive that time of year and you will see non-native pears, magnolia, spirea, forsythia, peaches, multiflora rose, quince, and daffodils pushing out fresh foliage or flowers, then along comes a late frost. Each region has its own progression on the calendar, but the plant families that thrive in those regions are remarkably the same in general appearance. They have, however, adapted themselves to the particular conditions through generations of natural selection.

# How to Use the Keys in This Book

Look for these icons for quick reference on where plants grow, seasons of use, and parts of the plant to reach for.

## LOCATION

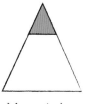
Mountains

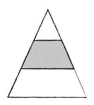
Piedmont

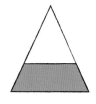
Coastal Plain

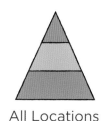
All Locations

## USEFUL PART OF PLANT

Fruit/Berries

Flowers

Seed Heads

Branches

Foliage

## SEASONS OF USE

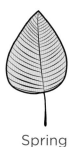
Spring

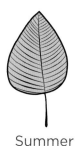
Summer

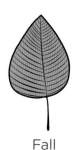
Fall

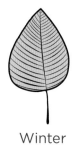
Winter

# Foraging

*The rules and tools of engagement*

# Conservation

The entire purpose of this book is to open your eyes to the native plants that are available for cutting and arranging. I am not, however, encouraging you to go out and pillage our shrinking plant communities. I want you to see them, love them, bring home a handful, and consider introducing them to your little patch of green, *not* drive them to extinction.

1. Step lightly, and if you must leave a path, let it be one of enlightenment. In areas where soils are thin, even one set of heavy human footprints can alter a plant community's terroir, and its recovery time could well be longer than your memory of traipsing through it.
2. *Never* cut more than one-third of the stems from any single plant—maintaining genetic diversity means leaving flowers open for cross pollination.
3. Don't even think about touching rare, endangered, or otherwise federally protected plants. It is illegal and just plain wrong. Karma will bite you in the butt if you do.
4. Don't dig up unusual plants in the hopes that they will go home to your garden and be happy. Chances are you will kill them, and then they are gone.
5. If you want to introduce local natives to your garden, harvest *some* seeds and leave the plant. Sow them in situ or try your hand in the greenhouse or a properly heated spot in your home. If you have ideal conditions for a particular species and obtain ripe seeds, they will eventually thrive, though they may take up to four years to show themselves.

# Where to Forage

Finding native plants to selectively harvest outside of the field or garden is easy if you keep your eyes and mind open to the possibilities. Native plants can be found virtually everywhere there is a place for them to put down a few roots, but the types one finds depends on the type of habitat they are growing in.

I have always joked that I am a familiar roadside sighting four seasons out of the year—spotted along ditches, slopes, and highway exits across the region, and have more than once pulled over or backtracked just to get a bit closer to something that caught my eye. Even if I don't need something at a particular time, I keep a mental tab on everything I see in case the need arises. Knowing my best sources makes it easier to get what I need when I do need it. Then I don't have to go out looking; I just go out and get it.

The paths most frequently taken are the ones that are harvested from the most. That is because everything that grows along those routes becomes memorized—when it blooms, when the foliage is just the right hue, when the berries are perfectly colored for my uses. Harvesting along familiar areas is also helpful in tracking how much of it there is year after year, so that the overall population of those favorites is maintained and not diminished.

## ROADSIDES

Surprisingly, the tough environments of roadsides are my go-to source for an abundant supply of some of the most important native "workhorse" cuts. These are the cut foliage, flowers, berries, and vines that are used personally and supplied to florists week after week throughout the growing season. They include sourwood, pokeweed, clematis, goldenrod, aster, and milkweed.

The roadside environment is a harsh one. The topsoil, if existent at all, is thin and low in nutrients, the sun may bake this hard soil all day if the trees have been cleared back, and the area is maintained by repeated mowing throughout the growing season. Plants along busy roadsides also have the added stress of breathing in excessive carbon monoxide and other emissions.

Ditches may often have sitting water for months on end, sprinkled with the lovely additions of beer cans, fast-food trash, and plastic bags and seasoned with whatever the Department of Transportation (DOT) lays down and cars spew out. From that springs forth surprising beauties like eupatorium, sarracenia, monarda, and myrica. Put your tall rubber boots on for this terrain!

Slopes can be rocky or clay-like and steep. They might be shockingly dry or have spring water seeping from them. Either way, basic physics determines that they are well drained. The sun may be relentless, or trees might tower above them and across the road, providing partial to full shade. Due to the specialized habitats that slopes tend to have, they are a favorite place to find native plants like gillenia, kalmia, and rubus.

Slopes are often unstable—try to climb some and everything can come tumbling down—the soil, the plants, and *you*. Be extremely cautious and considerate when harvesting from these areas. Don't climb! Use lightweight, telescoping pole pruners—then everything that needs to will stay put. You will most certainly want to return to these places, and you can't if you cause a mini landslide!

## FORESTS

Our forests are some of the most pristine areas to forage for native plants. Although the majority of them have had their trees cut down for timber at least once in the last two hundred years, their shady canopy has made a return, and the scars of rapid deforestation have slowly faded away. The remaining signs of our presence in the deep forest are the long-rotten stumps of giants, old logging roads and rail tracks for moving the harvest out, and the occasional fence post or chimney left behind by early settlers who couldn't make a life in that spot.

## CITIES AND SUBURBS

Locating native stems in a city or suburb is much easier than you might expect. It's all about knowing where to look. Nature always finds a way; even the tiniest crack in the concrete can play host to seeds that migrate into even the most populated, urbanized realms of a city.

Since I can't think of any cities in the Southeast that are truly concrete jungles—using a huge city such as Atlanta as a base of consideration—we have plenty to work with.

Green spaces abound, and variations in terrain provide unique habitats for distinct plants. Vacant lots, the "devil strip," overgrown property lines, railroad rights-of-way, and the green areas behind shopping centers are seemingly forgotten spaces that will surprise you with an array of some of the toughest plants around.

One of my favorite places to find surprises in developed areas is the back side of older shopping centers. Strips of buildings are erected, the surrounding area paved over for parking, and the requisite landscaping is installed to suit city and county codes. Storefronts are filled and opened with fanfare, people come, people go, and time passes. After a while, people stop coming as much—maybe there is a new place in town to go instead, and the maintenance budget goes down a bit. The doors of small businesses that seemed like a good idea at the time close and new ones fill their space. All the while, nature closes in: The long, protective hedge in the back, installed by the winning project bidder, slowly dies out and no one really seems to notice. Birds have been building nests in that hedge since it was planted and have pooped out enough seeds by now to start a forest. Those seeds fall down to the hardened soil beneath, which has been slowly enriched by shed foliage, where they germinate, take root, and are gently shaded by the old bushes—a perfect nursery in the concrete jungle. The hedge disappears as the vines rush up to the light, serving now as a trellis, though its giant gumdrop form persists beneath a scrambling green canopy of the winning survivor, whose roots have become one with the hedge and will never let go. Hurricane winds, winter, and the maintenance crew next door bring in perennial companions to the vines. No one notices—the original plan is long forgotten. Take a little cruise behind those places and you will find—erupting from a surface that is now thick with bottles and plastic shopping bags—native beauty: Greenbriar and grapevines, goldenrod and rabbit tobacco—these plants are living it up just a few feet away from belching freight trucks and employees on smoke breaks. Look past those green strip pioneers, maybe downhill to a defunct railroad track, and you'll find pokeberry, aster, and black-eyed Susans wrestling for space with the English ivy that has jumped the track from the bordering neighborhood.

Plants march along when no one is paying attention, and those spots are where you find the good stuff—tough enough to drape your doorways and halls without a word of complaint.

# Safety

I wouldn't be a very good foraging guide if I didn't talk about safety. These words are not intended to be discouraging in any way—it's always important for one to be aware of their surroundings and to stay safe. Some of these precautions are basic common sense and others you may have never considered. I have foraged in all kinds of places, and although I am always careful, I've been blindsided by a few things and paid for it in one way or another. Hopefully my experiences will prevent you from any unexpected discomfort.

Let's get the most unpleasant parts of this topic over with—the critters and plants that can make you hurt.

### STINGING AND BITING CRITTERS
The Hymenoptera family of insects includes several members that can pack a wallop with their sting, and some, like yellow jackets and bald-faced hornets, are very aggressive as a group when their hive is disturbed or even if they think you may disturb it. They will hunt you down! These species build large

nests either in the ground where you can't see them or hanging from branches that may not be noticeable until it's too late. They are most active midsummer through fall, but you should also be aware of the oversized queens seeking a place to nest in late spring. For those of you who have a known allergy to this family, don't walk out your door without an emergency treatment kit: EpiPen, antihistamines, and steroid medication if your doctor prescribes them for you.

## Saddleback Caterpillars

These aptly named little devils are no joke—even though I couldn't resist arranging a few I found in the nursery in a "roundup" formation (with a pencil) for their close-up photo. Stiff hairs on the body of this moth larvae secrete venom that delivers a painful punch if it comes into contact with skin, and I have been stung through two layers of clothing before. Saddlebacks are generally present late summer through fall, and they

*Saddleback caterpillars*

can be hard to spot since they are most often lurking on the underside of leaves of a wide range of species. I once had the misfortune of a face sting while harvesting some scrubby oak foliage. When I felt the pain, a quick check on the back of the foliage revealed a pinky fingernail–sized saddleback caterpillar. My advice? Look before you stick your face in bushes.

## Ticks and Spiders

Both of these groups are arachnids and have eight legs—as opposed to insects, which possess six legs. Tick bites can transmit disease, and the venom of black widow and brown recluse spiders may cause serious problems. Ticks wait for a host to pass by with their clingy little front arms waving about while their back ones hold onto a leaf or blade of grass. I haven't had a tick crawl onto me in over ten years because I wear fitted clothing and tall rubber boots, and tie my hair tight or don a hat when I'm in the woods. I also plan my woodland harvests for rainy days if possible. I think all of the above discourages ticks from grabbing hold as I pass by. Either that or they simply don't like me—which is just fine. If you are in an area that is known for ticks, strip and do a thorough tick search as soon as you get home. Deter spider bites by (a) dressing properly and (b) not sticking your hand in places you can't see. Black widows love to hang out underneath things, and brown recluses hide behind things. If you've cut some bushy stems to bring home, consider leaving them outside for the night so that any unwanted guests have the chance to crawl away.

*Snakes*

This region has its fair share of snakes, and they all play an important role in the ecosystem whether you like them or not, but none of us needs to suffer from a snakebite. Copperheads, cottonmouths (water moccasins), eastern coral snakes, and rattlesnakes are the venomous species of the Southeast, and you should always be on the lookout for them. These cold-blooded animals are active from April through October and are the most aggressive during their breeding season in autumn. Lessen your chances of a negative encounter: Look before you step, be extremely cautious near the water's edge, wear thick leather boots, listen for warning rattles, and, for goodness sake, don't stick your hands in places without looking first. If you do come across a snake that is coiled and ready to strike, back away slowly.

## POISONOUS FLORA

Hopefully by now you've learned the big three rash-inducing, misery-making plant species: poison ivy, poison oak, and poison sumac. Sensitivity varies from person to person—some are able to roll around in it and never have an itch whereas others seemingly only look at one of these species and break out in a rash. If you haven't already schooled yourself on these three common irritants, you definitely should before heading out to forage. You should also keep in mind that these woody plants contain just as much of these irritating compounds when they are dormant—if not more concentrated. Consider an accidental brush with the soft, watery foliage of the

*"Yes, it's pretty, but no, you can't handle it."*

growing season and multiply it several times to get the toxicity of a broken stem as it brushes your arm on a sunny late autumn day as you stretch to reach some pretty fence line berry stems.

Aside from the obvious "sticker bushes," a few other uncomfortable but not poisonous-to-the-touch plants worth mentioning are stinging nettle, horse nettle, and members of the hawthorn family. Familiarize yourself with the local environment; wear boots, gloves, and protective eyewear; and think before you touch.

## TERRAIN

Treading on sensitive terrain can cause damage to the ecosystem, but rough terrain can also cause damage to your person if you aren't careful. The sad truth is our forests are dying—faster than I ever dreamed. Aside from watching your step in all of the places I've mentioned, crossing over the carcasses of trees that were felled by fungus, disease, and wild swings in weather is another hazard. When a healthy tree falls from these events, the smaller branches are still strong. Give them a season or two and that remaining strong wood will sharpen itself into spears with the help of weather and gnawing creatures. Stepping or climbing over that felled ambassador to the plant world and hitting one of those sharpened branches can equal a stab wound on the leg. Falling on one and landing the wrong way could mean death. Mother Nature has a particular way of biting back.

## TRAFFIC

Sometimes I get caught up in the excitement of the hunt and forget the basics I learned as a youngster. If you are become a frequent forager, you may do the same. Here are a couple reminders:

Park your vehicle in a safe spot far enough away from passing traffic, but unless you are in a fully equipped four-wheel-drive expedition vehicle with some professional bogging tires, don't get too close to that ditch! If you see "Soft Shoulder" warning signs, don't leave the pavement.

Close the door of your vehicle when you stop and get out—an open driver's door on a roadside is usually a signal of someone in distress. It is also an open invitation for any and all curious passersby to stop and bother you. For your safety, keep a low profile.

## HERBICIDES

Both the DOT and utility companies periodically use herbicides to keep the vegetative growth down on roadsides and along power lines. There are two reasons you need to be aware of this: (1) No one needs to expose themselves to these chemicals if they don't have to, and (2) if you unwittingly harvest treated plants, they are going to turn into mush and possibly contaminate other stems when you get them home.

*Best practices for avoidance*
- Be alert to your surroundings: If wide bands of wilting or browned foliage are observed along roadsides and there isn't a drought, there's a good chance an herbicide has recently been applied. If you detect a chemical smell (other than passing vehicles), see trucks with tanks with liquid spraying from them or workers with backpack sprayers in these areas, wait until next year to harvest.
- If you are planning to forage in a particular area maintained by one of these entities and are concerned about herbicide residue, contact them and inquire of their spray schedule. Some power cooperatives post local spraying schedules on their websites.

**LEGALITIES**
- Don't trespass on private property. A simple knock on a door will go a long way.
- State and national forests allow the harvest of cut stems on non-threatened plant species for personal use without a permit. If it isn't for personal use, get a permit.
- DOT beautification and wildflower plantings are off-limits, and any idle state patrol officer will let you know just that if they see you. Signs are usually posted on the borders of those cultivated plantings.

## Tools for Harvesting

Good harvesting tools are essential to a forager's kit, and everybody has their favorites. I keep several sizes of the Japanese-made "ARS" hand pruners. The blades are a high-quality steel that stays sharp, and the smooth plastic handles are sturdy yet designed to be lightweight and comfortable enough to use for hours without exhausting my hands. Another thing I love about them is the handle color choices—ranging from pastels to white and classic red. Color may seem like a silly factor to consider, until you drop a pair into a sticker bush or they come out of your pocket by accident in an area of dense low growth or leafy forest floor.

- pruners
- loppers
- equipment for holding and transporting: buckets, open backpack, rubber bands
- clothing: boots, pants, long sleeves, gloves, eyewear
- bug spray

# Best Times for Harvest

Knowing when and how to harvest cut stems plays a crucial role in their vase life.

**MORNING AND EVENING**

Rule of thumb: Cut when temperatures are under 80°F. If your daytime temps are hovering around three digits and you are laughing at my mountain-centric rule of thumb—73°F at an altitude of 3,500 feet—wait for a nighttime cooldown. Cutting stems, flowering perennials and annuals in particular, is best done in either the morning or the evening. There are advantages to each. In the morning, plants are refreshed after a long dark break from the heat and better hydrated from the inevitable dew that gently covers them. In the evening plant sugars (their energy source) are more concentrated in the flowers. Cutting in the middle of a sunny day—*especially* when the thermometer reads over 80°F (or 90°F)—leaves you with stressed stems that may or may not recover. Avoid harvesting stems during or after very dry, windy conditions, as they are likely suffering from dehydration at those times.

**DURING OR RIGHT AFTER RAINFALL**

Yes, you will get wet, but harvesting during light rainfalls or right after a drenching downpour ensures that your stems are naturally hydrated and not suffering from stress. This is one of my favorite times to get "lost" in the woods; the colors seem brighter, and foliage has been washed of dust or pollen. Another advantage to getting wet is your skin and clothing becomes slick enough to deter crawling critters and thorny branches from grabbing on.

## STAGE OF HARVEST

Although there are exceptions to every rule, flowers, foliage, and berries each have basic windows within which they are at their best for cutting. Specific harvest stages are described by species in the field guide section of this book.

# Postharvest

Learning how to properly process cut stems after harvesting—the "postharvest" period—is another key to maximizing their vase life. When you return from foraging with buckets of goodies, it is important that you take the time to condition each stem before either arranging or temporarily storing them. There are basic steps that are easy to follow every time, and simple extra steps for woody, sappy, or just plain droopy stems that need a bit of extra postharvest care to ensure maximum hydration and vase life.

## THE BASICS

1. Get those pretty things out of the sweltering heat of a vehicle! Find a space to work in that is preferably cool and definitely out of direct sun. Stems need to cool down from any field heat and the car ride. If you don't have a garage or work room with a sink, the shade of a big tree and a garden hose, your kitchen sink, or even the shady side of a building will work just fine.

2. Use clean containers: Storage vessels—whether buckets or jars—need to be clean. I always tell my helpers that if the container isn't clean enough to put fresh vegetables in, it isn't clean enough for flowers. Bacteria, fungal spores, soil, or remaining plant residue in a container can shorten the vase life by inhibiting water uptake or causing rot. It's best to have your clean storage buckets ready upon your harvest return. You don't want to waste time scrambling for a clean container while your freshly cut stems stress themselves into a pile of wilted mush. In advance of harvesting—preferably after emptying them from their last use—scrub your containers inside and out with water and a few drops of bleach, then allow them to air dry completely before stacking and storing. They are then ready when you need them.

3. Provide an ideal water level: Fill your buckets with no more than 2 to 4 inches of fresh water. Most stems don't need to be submerged, as they generally take up water where they were cut. Too much water in the bucket can actually decrease water uptake. Cut stems drink the most water within 36 hours of harvesting, so keep an eye on the water level and add more accordingly.

4. Strip off leaves and recut the stems: Remove all foliage, flowers, or berries from the lower part of the stems to keep them out of the water and reduce crowding in the bucket. Recut the stems at an angle just before placing in the bucket—this reopens their vascular system, allowing for an unimpeded flow of water up the stem.

5. Don't overpack stems in a bucket, as decreased air flow around each stem can lead to stress and rot. This is more important in warmer temperatures—anything over 65°F. Overpacking also leads to unnecessary smooshing of your pretties as well as makes it difficult to pull out individual stems when you are arranging.

## EXTRA STEPS

Plants have vascular tissue like animals have a cardiovascular system. This tissue consists of both phloem and xylem. The phloem transports food up and down the plant's body depending on where the food source is and where it needs to be for storage or immediate use. For example, phloem can move sugars and amino acids from the leaves to the fruit or from a tuber to the growing tip. The xylem moves water and minerals up the stem from the roots. The upward motion of water within this tissue is important to understand because it directly affects how a stem behaves when cut. When the xylem tissue is exposed to air after being cut or broken, in self-preservation it immediately seals itself to prevent water from flowing out. Since in most instances we are working with actively growing material, we don't want that. Live stems need to be able to continuously take in more water to maintain both leaf and flower turgidity and also to keep unopened flowers on the path to opening.

Woody stems are able to take up more water if you follow these steps: First, make an extra cut to their stems. Hold the woody stem in one hand and with a sharp pair of clippers in the other, split the stem by making a vertical cut straight up the center—at least an inch long. Then make the regular diagonal cut. Secondly, plunge those stems into warm water. The warm water softens existing saps and natural oils and increases the flow of water upward.

Sappy or milky stem species, such as those in the milkweed family, exude either a milky-looking substance or sticky sap when they are cut. To keep them from drooping you have to prevent the substance from drying out and forming a seal at the cut end that blocks water uptake. This is best achieved by cutting the stem while it is submerged in warm water. The sap will flow out of the stem and allow water to flow in. If you cut the stem again for arranging, repeat this step.

Drooping stems: If the actual tissue isn't damaged, severely dehydrated stems may be rescued by cutting them while submerged in warm water. Re-cutting while submerged opens the vascular system so water may flow more freely into the stem. Cutting stems out of water causes the vascular system to close itself off from the end.

Hollow stems: Stems that are hollow need water in those stems to hold themselves upright. There are two ways of accomplishing this: (1) immediately turn the stem upside down in the water and make a cut, or (2) fill a tall, narrow bucket with water, recut the stem, and plunk it with intention into the water, forcing water into the stem. Allow stems to rest in a cool place for a couple of hours and then drain the water down to 4 inches.

## STORING CUT STEMS

Although it is best to use your harvest right after they have been hydrated for several hours, that isn't always possible—particularly if you are gathering a large amount over several days for an event. In that case, you'll need to store what you have until you are ready to use them. Keep in mind that not all species lend themselves to being held; some have a finite vase life and should be harvested at the last minute. For the rest, I suggest cold storage. Placing cut stems in cold storage (34–46°F)—either dry or in water—temporarily stops their growth, essentially suspending them in animation. A refrigerator works just fine, but if your fridge starts to hold more flowers than food on a regular basis, you may want to consider these options:

- **Used refrigerator:** These are a simple and inexpensive solution for storing cut flowers and foliage. It is important that you test it out first—if it doesn't function properly, you can end up with frozen mush.

- **Upright display cooler:** This is the kind of cooler you see in a convenience store stuffed full of soft drinks or sandwiches; good working used ones can be located and purchased in your area with a bit of sleuthing.

- **Walk-in cooler:** There are different versions of this type of cooler and they hold *a lot* of material, so they are best suited to full-time growers and florists to make the expense worthwhile.

If none of the above are practical, place cut stems in the coolest, darkest room you have for no more than two days.

# *Plants*

## *A Flower Forager's Field Guide to Native Plants of the Southeast*

This is a field guide of excellent native workhorses that are either easily found throughout all sub-regions or are more particular and frequent to particular regions. It certainly doesn't cover all of the species I use, but this is a beginning point. Once your eyes are opened, you will be amazed at the possibilities that will jump out and call your name.

# PERENNIALS, BIENNIALS, AND ANNUALS

PERENNIALS ARE HERBACEOUS NON-WOODY PLANTS that return year after year after a period of dormancy. Biennials are plants that generally flower a year after the seed germinates and then die. Annuals are individual plants that complete their entire life cycle within a year. As a group, these flowering plants are the youngest in the chain of evolution and are by far the most numerous and diverse. Since each generation of these plants reaches productive maturity relatively quickly, they are able to respond and adapt to different growing conditions, and therefore evolve into different species and subspecies within a much smaller time frame than trees and shrubs. Species that produce large amounts of seed are highly responsive to their environments, and that is why you see such variation from one area to the next. Aster and goldenrod are good examples of this. Other species, like pokeweed, seem to be happy no matter where they are, and are relatively consistent wherever they are found. Why do some groups change so much while others stay relatively the same from one environment to the next? My guess is they have developed differing mechanisms of survival and distribution. Those that rely on wind and water to move their small seeds from one place to the next seem to have a higher rate of regional variability and diversification, while those that rely on birds and mammals to transport their big seeds seem more consistent.

Regardless of these scientific musings, perennials, biennials, and annuals provide a treasure trove of beautiful cut stems from one season to the next.

## *Achillea millefolium*

### Yarrow

The flat-topped flowering heads of yarrow are held above pleasantly scented ferny foliage by strong, slightly hairy stems. Flowers are usually white, but I've seen shades of light pink in the wild as well. Yarrow is a tough plant that dislikes excess water or shade. Deer won't touch it, which is a *huge* bonus for us. Yarrow makes a great garden plant in sunbaked areas with lower humidity. Modern species selection and hybrids have increased their color diversity.

## USES

Yarrow makes a great filler in arrangements or can hold its own when it is the exclusive subject. Yarrow has a place in dried designs given its strong stems and resistance to crumbling, although the colored varieties tend to dull more than the white.

## HARVEST

Yarrow is best harvested in the early morning before the dew has evaporated. The flowers should have visible pollen on them—if cut at an earlier stage, wilting is likely and difficult to reverse.

## POSTHARVEST

Stems may be held in a cooler for up to ten days without damage. Vase life is five to ten days.

# Anemone virginiana

*Thimbleweed, Wild Anemone*

The one- to two-inch, glistening white flowers of wild anemone are the shape of a broad star with five sepals. A golden (fading to brown) corona of pollen surrounds the green pistil head, which eventually becomes the "thimble" of the common name.

The generally three-lobed, serrated leaves are concentrated at the base of this perennial. Although bright green in the summer, they may emerge in spring with a purple cast to them—especially in soil low in phosphorous.

## USES

Borne on long, thin stems, both the flowers and green heads provide a light, vertical component to summer arrangements that may otherwise appear overly heavy with the abundance of high summer. The green thimbles also make great textural additions to boutonnieres.

## HARVEST

Harvest flowers in bud, partially to fully opened, and thimbles as soon as the petals drop and as long as the head stays firm and green.

## POSTHARVEST

Vase life is up to a week for stems with flowers and buds and up to a month for the thimbles. Floral preservative is recommended for flowers that are not fully opened at harvest time.

# *Aquilegia canadensis*
## Columbine

Our native columbine is easily distinguished by its red lantern-shaped flowers with a center cup of yellow. The short-lived perennials appear in spring above blue-green foliage resembling that of maidenhair fern. They are most often found growing in the rocky crevices of slopes and roadside banks where there is some sunlight and little competition. Be cautious when you find a patch—I always seem to find columbine growing near poison ivy (which is dormant when they are blooming)—likely because both gravitate toward areas where other vegetation is sparse.

### USES

The thin, delicate stems of columbine make them best used in light, airy arrangements paired with anything else you can find in the early days of spring. Consider using both flowers and foliage mixed with one or two other spring ephemerals in a grouping of tiny vases.

### HARVEST

Cut stems when there are both open flowers and buds on the stem.

### POSTHARVEST

Stems with multiple blooms of early season flowers will last a week in water. Stems can be held at 36°F for one to two weeks; however, vase life will be shortened.

# *Aruncus dioicus*

Goat's Beard, Bride's Feathers

The airy ivory flowers of goat's beard appear to float above the deep green compound pinnate foliage after the spring flowers have finished blooming but before many of the summer flowers appear. This makes them all the more distinctive on the north-facing slopes they favor because the world around them is a sea of green. It is interesting to note that the species name *dioicus* is derived from the Greek words *di* ("two") and *oikos* ("house"), so "two houses," because goat's beard plants are either male or female, not both. In the garden, goat's beard may take awhile to become established, but this five-inch-tall perennial is tough and long lived if it is situated in a cool, shady spot with well-drained, moist soil.

## USES

Goat's beard flowers bring nonpareil lightness to large arrangements and are perfect for wedding work. Mix with greens, clear blues, pinks, and peaches.

Similar to later-blooming *Astilbe* 'Bridal Veil,' which looks downright coarse when compared to *Aruncus*.

**HARVEST**
I prefer to cut stems before the flowers open—they are less prone to breakage then, and if you are using them outdoors, the tiny pollinators that favor them will stay away.

**POSTHARVEST**
Goat's beard can be stored in a cooler at 38–42°F for up to a week if given plenty of open-air space (a walk-in cooler). Otherwise, I do not recommend cold storage. Vase life is up to eight days if cut in bud stage.

# *Asclepias* Species

## The Milkweeds

Milkweeds live up to their common name due to the white sap in many of the species that bleeds out wherever the plant's tissue is disturbed. The individual flowers of every milkweed I've encountered remind me of ladies in skirts doing the can-can dance. There are around thirty straight species of milkweed growing in the Southeast and almost as many subspecies described. To me, that much diversity within a single genus indicates the vital role it plays in the ecosystem. It is the preferred source of nectar for mature monarch butterflies, and the foliage is consumed voraciously by their caterpillars. Countless other Lepidoptera species can also be observed feasting when they are in bloom. What does that mean for the native florist? Harvest sparingly in the wild, and plant some in your garden for the butterflies. If you encounter a local milkweed you like, never, ever dig it up because chances are good that you will kill it. Make a note of its location and allow yourself one seed pod to start in your own garden. If there is only one pod, allow it to dry and open on the plant, and then gather no more than one-third of the seeds in the pod.

# *Asclepias exaltata*
## Poke Milkweed

Poke milkweed can be found in groups growing on shady, moist banks in early summer. Its soft, wide leaves, which resemble those of *Phytolacca* (pokeweed), give it the common name.

### USES
This milkweed's sweet scent and dusty, lilac-kissed white flowers make it a pretty addition to natural pastel designs. Works well with blueberries, sourwood, and silver foliage.

### HARVEST
Cut poke milkweed when half of the flowers in the floppy cluster look like can-can dancers (as opposed to the unopened ball-shaped buds). The stems must immediately go into water. If possible, cut the stems underwater right after you harvest them.

### POSTHARVEST
Cut stems under warm water and repeat if necessary to achieve full hydration. Vase life is a week after hydrated. Stems can be stored in a cooler for no more than a week.

# *Asclepias syriaca*
## Common Milkweed

This is a tough species of milkweed that spreads by underground rhizomes to form large colonies if in an ideal spot in sunny pastures and roadsides. They seem to like areas that are regularly cleared of other vegetation via mowing, although good luck trying to take these hefty babes down with a rotating blade less than one fit for cutting hay with a tractor.

## USES

The round clusters of light dusty mauve flowers smell heavenly and look good paired with other muted shades. Tuck them into low centerpieces or at the bottom of larger designs. The seedpods bring interesting textural drama and heft to late season compositions, or can be dried for wreath work in fall and winter.

## HARVEST

This hefty milkweed should be cut when about half of the flowers are open in the cluster, and immediately cut again under warm water. Otherwise, you may not be able to rehydrate any droopy ones. For dried pods, cut them as soon as they have filled out and hardened slightly. If you wait too long, they are likely to split open—revealing seeds that float away on a puff of silky fiber. The split pods may be interesting to use as well.

## POSTHARVEST

Once the stems are fully hydrated, they can be used, but if you cut them again when designing, do it underwater. Flowering stems can be held for a week in a cooler for immediate use; vase life is up to five days. Seedpods can be dried upright in a bright, warm, well-ventilated spot for at least two weeks.

# *Asclepias tuberosa*

## Butterfly Milkweed

The bright orange flowers of this species make them easy to spot throughout the area on hot, sunny, dry roadsides and other open areas such as power line clearings and pastures. Their flower show begins in May and moves through June and even July in the cooler regions. Unlike other milkweed species, butterfly milkweed doesn't have a strong flow of milky sap when cut, and therefore does not need to be drained of sap to prevent drooping. The species name *tuberosa* refers to the meaty taproot that sustains the plant below the soil's surface. It is important to note that if the taproot is broken or damaged in any way, it will delay flowering for a year or more, so don't even think about trying to dig one up. If you wish to cultivate them, their seeds are easily gathered and spread once the oblong seed capsule shows signs of splitting open. Start them in small pots and then plant once they are a manageable size. Be very gentle in handling the seedlings when transplanting.

### USES

Stems can be cut long or short and work well in vases, bouquets, and boutonnieres. The shape and size of the flower heads varies by plant, and the more open ones can add a cascading effect to smaller arrangements if placed thoughtfully. They add an unexpected flower shape to monochromatic compositions, and the bright orange pairs well with chartreuse, white, fuchsia, and any shade of blue or purple.

### HARVEST

Stems can be cut when one-quarter of the buds have opened until all are opened. Plants that are removed of all flowering stems will send out more flowers in the same season and can be considered a late season source of nectar for migrating monarchs.

### POSTHARVEST

Place recut stems into air temperature water. Floral preservative may be added and extends vase life by three days. Stores well in a 42°F cooler for up to five days. Vase life is five to nine days depending on the stage harvested and whether or not floral preservative is used.

# *Aster* Species

When the days become shorter, members of the aster tribe cover themselves with small, delicately rayed flowers that wink at you with yellow eyes. They carpet and drape down banks and roadsides in so much abundance, floating like white, blue, and lavender mist over seasonally fading greens, weaving themselves through the goldenrods and suntanned grasses. This highly diverse group of species and subspecies once fell in the common genus *Aster*. Recently though, taxonomists have busied themselves re-categorizing them into separate genera based on their DNA and physical characteristics: *Ampelaster*, *Doellingeria*, *Eurybia*, *Oclemena*, *Seriocarpus*, and *Symphyotrichum*. They are grouped here as members of the "aster tribe" and are commonly referred to as such.

## USES
Aster flowers bring the lightness of an autumn sky to seasonal compositions that are often dominated by warm tones. Mix them with the goldenrods and

*Aster—Eurybia macrophylla*

flowering grasses they bloom alongside, and add peachy dahlias, changing foliage, and trailing clematis.

**HARVEST**
Aster stems can be cut beginning when about half of the individual flowers have opened and until they begin to fade.

**POSTHARVEST**
Place cut aster stems into warm water to hydrate for a couple of hours if needed, or use immediately. Vase life depends on species and stage of harvest, but expect four to eight days.

# *Baptisia australis*

Blue Wild Indigo

# *Baptisia lanceolata*

Gopher Weed

*Baptisia* species, or "false indigo," is a tough, long-lived perennial that makes its home throughout the region. Many of these members of the legume family rocket out of the ground from crowns with deep taproots in early spring, with indigo-toned spikes that look somewhat like asparagus. They quickly become long, elegant spires of white, blue, or yellow flowers topping rounded blue-green foliage. Gopher weed possesses the same beautiful glaucous foliage, but its yellow flowers are not arranged on a spike, rather are held in groups of four to five, just past the more oblong olive-green foliage of this rounded form. My favorite species is *Baptisia alba*, which has long, thin spires of pure white flowers on blue stems.

Over the last several years, there has been a boom in baptisia breeding, which has produced nativars in not only a wide range of colors but also plant sizes, from purple-flowered varieties that can reach 4 or 5 feet down to a pink one that is only about 2 feet tall. There are even several varieties that have interesting brown- to black-colored flowers. Given that range, there is a baptisia for every garden.

*Baptisia australis*

*Baptisia lanceolata*

## USES

Baptisia are excellent cut flowers—the taller varieties bring a spired elegance to large bouquets, tall centerpieces, and large installations. Smaller-flowered varieties can be the focal points in arrangements set in vases as small as a wineglass. Pair them with other spikes, airy fillers, and softly textured garden roses and use the foliage as a base. The blue-green foliage is an excellent replacement any time of the growing season for eucalyptus as long as it is kept hydrated. As it begins to age to yellow, use it to bring a soft glow to autumn compositions. The sooty black seed pods make a great textural addition to designs.

## HARVEST

Flowers are best harvested beginning when two-thirds of the flowers have opened and until the spike is completely filled out. If you don't need tall stems, cut only the central flower on the stalk and save the smaller side flowers until they mature, or leave them to produce seeds. Foliage can be cut as soon as the flowers have matured and until it goes dormant. Seedpods may be harvested as soon as they have blackened.

**POSTHARVEST**

Cut both flower and foliage stems in warm water. Vase life is about six days. My testing has shown that the flowers can be stored in a 38–42°F cooler for up to three weeks if they are cut in the earlier (half-filled) stage, but vase life will be reduced by half.

# *Conoclinium coelestinum*

Blue Mistflower, Ageratum

Wild ageratum has clusters of fuzzy flowers in a fine shade of plumbago blue—like the morning sky with its hints of purple. It is most visible in wetter roadside ditches beginning in late summer. The sometimes-red stems can add another level of color interest. Unlike its introduced annual cousin—ageratum—that looks strikingly similar in flower, this one is truly hardy to zone 6.

**USES**

Use in anything—it holds well in most conditions (except for drying), and we all need a little blue sometimes. I like pairing it with purple and chartreuse, and it is always wonderful with white or yellow.

**HARVEST**

Cut stems when the flowers look fuzzy. Do not cut when in bud—it will droop and is not only hard to bring back at that stage, but the buds aren't likely to open.

**POSTHARVEST**

Vase life can be up to ten days *if* water is changed and floral preservative is used. This species' proclivity for growing in slightly swampy conditions seems to make it one that can create a swamp wherever it is (stinky flower water warning!).

# *Coreopsis lanceolata*

Lanceleaf Tickseed

# *Coreopsis verticillata*

Whorled Tickseed

Coreopsis are a bright group of plants that thrive in sunny spots from dry to swampy, depending on the species, along roadsides and in open forests throughout the region. Most species have yellow flowers with either a yellow or dark brown eye, but there is also a pink species—*Coreopsis nudata* (Georgia tickseed) that is found on the coastal plain of Georgia and Florida. I would really like to get my hands on the pink one!

**USES**

Whether the coreopsis you are using has large or small flowers, its thin stems and light petals bring a golden (or pink) floating quality to any seasonal arrangement. Best in water.

*Coreopsis lanceolata*

*Coreopsis verticillata*

**HARVEST**

Cut stems that have many flowers when about half of them are open. Cut stems with one to four flowers once the central flower opens and pollen is evident.

**POSTHARVEST**

The stems of *Coreopsis* species with large numbers of flowers can last in a vase for up to ten days. The larger-flowered species, when cut with unopened buds, can last up to seven days.

# *Eupatorium* Species

There are so many species of eupatorium that even I have difficulty discerning them at times. They are a valuable nectar source for a wide array of flying insects. Found across the region, their different forms inhabit a variety of growing conditions—from the deep shade on the north side of mountains to the baking-hot sandhills of the coast. Wherever they are found, the late season blooms provide interesting texture and soft varied shades for floral design.

# *Eupatorium capillifolium*

Dog Fennel

Dog fennel is the most unusual looking of this genus. The light green shoots with needle-like leaves and a strong herby scent grow straight up from the ground and have a slightly prehistoric look as they approach 4 to 5 feet. In autumn myriad tiny flowers transform the appearance of this oddball with a tawny cascade of smoky fluff.

**USES**

Dog fennel lends a romantic softness to any large bouquet, centerpiece, or arbor arrangement in autumn. Consider using it as a flexible replacement for pampas grass plumes. Pair with rich orange shades, copper, brick, and even dusty pink.

**HARVEST**

Harvest once the flowers are evident above the foliage in autumn. There is a definite change in texture to the plant when they are ready to bloom.

**POSTHARVEST**
Use immediately or store in a cooler to delay flower opening. Vase life is six days if cut in bud.

# *Eupatorium perfoliatum*

Boneset

This species earned its common name from the old belief that it could be used as a remedy to repair broken bones because of the way the opposite leaves are set at strong 90-degree angles from the stem. Although it turns out boneset isn't going to fix any broken bones, its properties have been shown to be a powerful remedy for the influenza virus. Aside from the strong-looking foliage, boneset can be distinguished from the other large eupatorium with dome-shaped flower heads by its white flowers that are strongly set on only slightly rounded dome-shaped heads atop 2- to 5-foot-tall plants. There are other white eupatorium species, and most of them have similar uses.

## USES

Boneset is great as a sturdy yet subtle white filler in late summer for any type of arrangement.

## HARVEST

Harvest when the flower buds appear and until they begin to dull with age.

## POSTHARVEST

If boneset is harvested in bud stage, it can last for up to fourteen days, even in a bucket of water sitting in full blazing sun. Stems can also be dried sitting upright in a container placed in a warm, dry spot with filtered light.

# *Eupatorium fistulosum, E. purpureum,* and *E. maculatum*

## Joe Pye Weed

Joe pye weed is an unmistakable presence in the landscape with its towering domes of mauve-colored flowers. Some say that when it begins to bloom, summer is coming to a close. Note that taxonomists have recently changed this group to the genus *Eutrochium*, but since these species are still known in the trade as eupatorium, that is how they are referred to here.

These plants have such an incredible presence when they are blooming and have been incorporated beautifully into both formal and loose "prairie style" (by famed Dutch designer Piet Oudolf) designs. Thanks to his pioneering work, it and many other beautiful North American native species have slowly gained recognition as garden worthy, and even the straight species are available commercially. It goes to show that our most beautiful North American natives still have to go to finishing school in Europe to gain legitimacy on this side of the ocean.

*Eupatorium fistulosum*

## USES

Joe pye weed is a wonderful addition to late summer compositions of any size. The full heads provide a mauvy-hazed backdrop for warmer tones in both large arrangements and installations, and they can also be parceled down by cutting the individually stemmed clusters to tuck into work as small as a boutonniere. The color works with cool tones as well, but in August, that just seems out of place. If you must, mix with white, clear pinks, and pistachio. Better though, are mixes with gold, terracotta, salmon, peach, dusty rose, and chartreuse to lime greens—just sayin' . . .

## HARVEST

Cut flower stems in proportion to planned use (but no longer than 4 feet) when all of the buds have filled out and are firm at the top of the inflorescence.

## POSTHARVEST

Strip the lower leaves and cut stems at a diagonal. May be stored in a cooler at 36–42°F for up to five days for fresh-cut sales and bouquets, and up to two weeks if being used for short-lived work like weddings and parties.

## *Euphorbia corrolata*

Flowering Spurge

Flowering spurge holds airy sprays of tiny, pure white flowers above long stems with bluish-green foliage. This under-recognized perennial deserves to be included in the cut flower repertoire for its crystalline flowers that can serve as a sophisticated replacement for baby's breath. It also serves as a tough garden plant that shrugs off heat and drought.

## USES

Mix flowering spurge with other whites in medium to

large designs that need a lighter touch. Honestly, what doesn't white go with? The sky is the limit!

## HARVEST
Like milkweeds, spurges emit a milky sap that may cause skin irritation when exposed to sunlight. Cut stems when most of the flowers are open on the stalk and place directly in water to flush away the sap.

## POSTHARVEST
Flowering spurge will flourish in clean water for seven days or more. Cold storage is not recommended.

# *Euthamia caroliniana*
Slender Goldenrod

# *Euthamia graminifolia*
## Flat Top Goldenrod

These species are not true goldenrods, and there isn't anything rod-like about them. This politely spreading perennial's 3- to 4-foot vertical stems with narrow leaves are topped with golden yellow, umbel-shaped clusters in late summer through autumn. Several years ago, I brought a small clump of *Euthamia caroliniana* from my family's zone 8b coastal plain back to our zone 6 North Carolina mountain garden and planted it in the border to see what would happen. It continues to thrive as a slowly expanding clump without any winter protection. It usually manages to explode into flower at least two weeks before a killing frost arrives and is the last hooray for my perennial garden. *Euthamia graminifolia* occurs naturally in the mountains, spreads more aggressively on roadside banks, and is typically finished before September in the area.

### USES
Add this pretty genus to any late season arrangement. It is a great substitute for goldenrod if a different shape is needed, but can also be paired with it and other yellows for spectacular monochromatic combinations. Balance out with purple ironweed, orange zinnias, and dahlias in large vases, or use it as a visually lightweight yet sturdy filler in large installations.

### HARVEST
Cut stems when they begin to glow yellow before the flowers open and until the color begins to dull.

### POSTHARVEST
Place cut stems into warm water and use within a day or two. Vase life is up to nine days.

# *Galax urceolata*
## Beetleweed

The galax of southern Appalachia is unique in that it is the sole species of the genus. That means there is truly nothing else like it—anywhere. For generations, the glossy, round, dark green to burgundy (winter color) foliage has made it popular enough with florists all over the world to send people into the woods to gather it in bulk and sell it to brokers. The brokers sell it up the supply chain, and ultimately those pretty leaves end up in the hands of florists as far away as Holland and Japan. Because of its seemingly vast plentitude, harvesting in state and national forests has historically been allowed, with a permit.

Traditionally, the largest leaves are gathered from plants and the rest is left intact, maintaining the slow-growing plant for future generations to harvest. After a blitz of internet research on the species, I was dismayed to learn that local galax populations are being rapidly decimated in the area where it is most common—western North Carolina. Poachers are trekking deep into the forest from the Blue Ridge Parkway, pulling entire plants out of the ground by the hundreds, cutting the valuable leaves, and dropping the carcasses—roots and all—on the ground to die. After learning that, I was hesitant to list galax as a harvestable native, but after considerable thought, I decided to use it to illustrate

how species may seemingly disappear without reason and our role as conservators. I cannot reiterate strongly enough the rules of engagement: tread lightly, don't be greedy. We want these plants to be there when we return and when our children return after us.

## USES
The thin, white spires of galax flowers are a sweet addition to boutonnieres and add a light vertical note to small compositions. The shiny, rounded foliage adds a grounding base of greenery to low centerpieces.

## HARVEST
Leaves may be cut from the plant when they are deep green and have fully hardened off in the summer, and through winter when they have turned a burgundy purple. Flowers can be cut in late spring, but only sparingly so as to maintain a natural seed stock.

## POSTHARVEST

Foliage can be stored cold for a month. Vase life for foliage is twelve days or longer if allowed to slowly dry. Flower vase life is ten days, and cold storage for up to ten days is possible.

# *Gillenia trifoliata*

## Bowman's Root, Indian-Physic

Gillenia is a tough perennial with starry white flowers hovering loosely above attractive, serrated trifoliate leaves on strong, wiry stems. They can be found hanging from slopes in sunny to shady rocky areas. It is also a lovely garden perennial in zone 7 or lower. I fell in love with this plant years ago when I found a stand of them on a high mountain road near Boone, North Carolina. Now that my eyes are trained for them, I spot them throughout the season from 1,800 to 5,600 feet elevation. The interesting thing about this species is that it is virtually unknown in the United States, but in Europe it is grown and harvested by a handful of specialty cut-flower growers and auctioned at *the* flower market in Holland. Dutch landscape designers and home gardeners have incorporated it into their gardens as well. Several years ago, an unidentified bareroot plant arrived in a bag of Holland-grown lily bulbs, and I planted it to see what it was. As soon as the leaves emerged I knew it was gillenia, and it is now a 3.5-foot-tall specimen in my perennial border. Highly recommended as a garden plant in the cooler climates of the region—if you can find it.

## USES

The fluttery white flowers of gillenia bring a unique movement to any arrangement, especially since they have such a wonderful backdrop of foliage. Pair with the light yellows of golden alexander (zizia), flowering dill, and the spiky soft mauves and pinks of *Verbascum* 'Southern Charm,' and bring deep velvety elegance to the whole thing by adding the rounded foliage of *Cotinus* 'Purple Smoke.' Works beautifully in all white compositions as well—especially with mock orange.

## HARVEST

Stems can be harvested as soon as the flowers appear and can continue through the seed head stage.

## POSTHARVEST

Vase life is ten days. Will hold in a 38°F cooler for two weeks (or more) as long as there are unopened flowers on the stems

# *Gnaphalium obtusifolium*

## Rabbit Tobacco

Rabbit tobacco makes itself evident in early autumn about the same time as goldenrod. Its straight stems are topped with flat flower heads, and every part of it veritably shines with shades of ivory to gray, making them distinctive in the season's wild landscape. Its pleasant mellow herbal scent plus unique color and texture endure for a couple of months while standing in the sunny dry spot they choose to grow in as the plant world around them goes from green to orange to brown. It is likely that these traits made this plant the first one I ever recall noticing on my own. I distinctly remember asking an adult what it was and receiving the answer "rabbit tobacco." I immediately imagined a bunch of teenage rabbits smoking behind a building. I was only around five or seven and loved *Peter Rabbit* stories. I suppose that's a good way to remember just about anything: visualize something familiar and attach a bit of scandal to it.

As a grownup, I've found this plant indispensable in my fall lineup—both fresh and dried.

## USES

Single stems add a pearlescent note to just about anything in autumn—pair with burgundy/blacks, terracotta, peach, and dusty pinks along with the

changing foliage of the season. Excellent for wreath work on its own or with other long-lasting dried components.

## HARVEST

Cut stems in the fall when the flowers are still tight, pointy buds. Do not over-harvest any given area of this plant, or you will not have anything to return to the following season.

## POSTHARVEST

If being used for dried creations such as wreaths, hang-dry individually wrapped bunches on a vertical line in a warm, dry space—a greenhouse or old tobacco barn is a good choice—for two weeks. Store either upright or carefully packed in dry bins until use.

# *Helianthus* Species

The Latin bases for this genus are *helio* ("sun") and *antho* ("flower"). The large majority of sunflower species are native to North America, and about half of those are perennial. They begin to bloom when the days are long and continue into autumn, each species offering up its little suns to the sky in a procession that lasts for weeks. There are quite a few useful species throughout the Southeast, and a few favorites are highlighted, but I encourage you to locate and try out the best in your area.

## *Helianthus angustifolius*
### Swamp Sunflower

This species produces great clusters of flowers in the fall on tall plants. They spread by underground rhizomes, so if you plant them in your garden, you'll have some clumps to share with friends in two or three years.

## *Helianthus radula*
### Rayless Sunflower

This neat little coastal plain species is a great substitute for black scabiosa and chocolate cosmos, which don't love growing there. It also makes a lovely dried flower.

## *Helianthus strumosus*
### Woodland Sunflower

This species of tall growers begins to show in July. Plants like dry soil and can be found in scattered areas throughout the region along open woodland edges.

## *Helianthus tuberosus*
### Sunchoke

Originating from the Great Plains, sunchokes were slowly scattered eastward by Native Americans, who cultivated them for their tasty tubers; when cooked, they taste like artichokes. A

word to the wise—although they are entirely safe to eat, not everybody has a digestive system that can handle them, which is when the letter *f* can be added to the beginning of the word "artichoke." Although I am one of the unlucky, I absolutely love their pale yellow flowers that appear in the fall. This species is almost too easy to grow, and the flowers alone are worth it.

## USES

Sunflowers can act as either the focal point or as sideline players to any summer to fall arrangement. Pair with goldenrod, liatris, and echinacea for a classic combo; work in with rosy brown shades plus a hint of blue set in amber glass for a striking autumn display; or keep it monochromatic by gathering every yellow flower you can find and setting them all into a base of pine branches.

## HARVEST

Cut stems are best harvested in the early morning just after the pollen appears. If there are multiple flowers, make sure the first one is at that stage.

## POSTHARVEST

Sunflowers have natural oils in the stems and can be tricky to hydrate. Cut stems under warm water and allow a night to fully hydrate if they are droopy.

# *Lepidium virginicum*

## Pennycress, Pepper Grass

Pennycress is a sweet little annual in the mustard family that can be distinguished from its more aggressive cousins by its flat, circular seed capsules (penny-shaped) that whorl densely below tiny white flowers on lightweight stems. The floral industry has taken note of its appeal, and it is cultivated by both small flower farms and commercial growers alike. I let it grow itself on my farm—allowing it to sow here and there, wherever my discarded stems land and drop their seeds. I have never considered it as a weed

or uninvited guest, and can easily find extras by visiting the edges of pastures and fields.

## USES
Pennycress can be used either fresh or dried. Fresh stems provide an airy, green mist effect to arrangements and blend well with white, pale yellow, or light pink flowers. The light strength also makes it great for wreaths—a fully rounded effect requires only a handful of stems.

## HARVEST
Pennycress can be cut for fresh use when they are at a ratio of about half and half seed to flower. For dried use, cut them after the tiny white flowers are no longer visible.

## POSTHARVEST
Fresh stems can last a week in a vase or be stored in a cooler for up to a week. Dried stems last indefinitely, but may become ratty after a year or two.

# *Liatris* Species

Gayfeather, Blazing Star

There are multiple species of liatris scattered across the southeastern United States— each filling a particular niche depending on climate and soil conditions. Their many tiny lilac-colored flowers bloom from the top down on long skinny spikes, setting themselves apart from anything else around them. They populate dry, sunny, open areas from sandy to clay soils and, depending on the species, bloom from midsummer into autumn. The commercial floral industry has adopted hybrids of liatris that have bulkier heads than the native species, but I prefer the lightness of our natives.

## USES
Incorporate liatris wherever a vertical spiky element is needed. It pairs well with orange

lilies, golden yellow flowers, and shades of peach. Dried stems can be tucked into autumn wreaths and arrangements for a soft pop of lavender.

## HARVEST

For fresh use, cut stems when the flowers at the top of the spike open. For dried use, cut when about half of the length of flowers are open.

## POSTHARVEST

Use fresh or store in a cooler for up to one week. Vase life is seven to fourteen days. For dried stems, place upright in a container in a dry room or barn that receives some—preferably morning—light.

# *Lilium superbum*

## Turk's Cap Lily

Turk's cap lilies are one of the biggest highlights of the midsummer bloom. They can form large, showstopping colonies numbering in the hundreds. Their flowers have a distinct green star in the center, with brown spotting on the upwardly curving orange petals. Anywhere from two to over a dozen flowers are held in an open pyramid on top of stems towering 4 to 10 feet (yes!) tall. The leaves are about five times longer than they are wide, with the widest part at the center, and they whorl all the way around the stem at 6- to 8-inch intervals starting from a foot off the ground up to the beginning of the inflorescence.

These features are all important to note because it distinguishes them from the endangered and protected (meaning *don't touch*!) Carolina lily—*Lilium michauxii*. Carolina lilies never have more than one or two flowers, do not have a green star in the very center of the flowers, and have shorter foliage (three to one length vs. width), which is widest toward the tip of the leaf, on top of short 1- to 4-foot plants. I have observed that Carolina lilies bloom slightly later than the Turk's cap lilies do in the same area.

If you are fortunate enough to come across a plentiful stand of Turk's cap lilies, it is okay to harvest a couple in most of the Southeast except Florida—where they are endangered, and Kentucky—where they are threatened.

## USES
Make one tall stem the spectacular centerpiece in a large natural arrangement. Pairs well with the tall stems of pokeweed and *Verbena hastata*. Since they are often flowering in close proximity, Turk's cap lilies also pair well with bright red or fuchsia flowers of bee balm (*Monarda didyma*).

## HARVEST
In order to enjoy these majestic flowers for the longest time possible, harvest when the first flower at the bottom of the pyramid begins to open. For balance in a tall vase, make sure you cut stems at least 1 to 2 feet below the lowest bloom.

## POSTHARVEST
Single flowers open daily and last about three to four days apiece (beginning at the bottom and moving to the top of the pyramid), so vase life depends on how many flowers are on the stalk. Stems with many unopened buds can be stored successfully in a cooler for up to four weeks at 38°F, but after two weeks, they will slowly begin to open in the cooler.

# *Lobelia siphilitica*
## Blue Lobelia, Fan Flower

Finding pure blue flowers in mid- to late summer is always a challenge, and I was overjoyed when I figured out just how well this lobelia species does as a cut flower. Their pure blue flowers are shaped like tiny fans—hence the common name—and are held up and down light, vertical stems. Blue lobelia can be spotted in partly to fully sunny low-lying areas near creeks, rivers, ponds, and bogs. Another species—*Lobelia amoema*—can be found farther south.

## USES

Longer stems can be used as a replacement for delphinium in arrangements, and shorter stems can be tucked into bouquets for a bit of blue.

## HARVEST

Cut stems when half of the flowers are open up the stalk.

## POSTHARVEST

Vase life is ten days, and benefits from floral preservative in the water. Can be stored in a cooler for up to seven days.

# *Lupinus perennis*

## Sundial Lupine

Several species of lupine occur throughout the Southeast, and this one is my favorite. It is most easily found in the coastal plain area and is easily distinguished by both floral display and foliage. Lupine is a member of the large

legume/pea family (Fabaceae) and therefore possesses the ability to fix its own nitrogen via a symbiotic relationship with beneficial *Rhizobium* bacteria that inhabits nodules within the root system. If you were to pull one of these plants out of the ground (good luck—their taproots don't let go of the earth very easily), the round nodules would be quite visible.

## USES
Native lupine has shorter stems than the cultivated perennial hybrids (which do not like to grow in most of the sweltering Southeast), and therefore lend themselves to small arrangements. Mix with pine branches and *Phlox pillosa*.

## HARVEST
Harvest sparingly when about half of the flowers are open along the stem because you want these babes to produce seeds and make more! Lupine stems need to be plunked with purpose into a water bucket immediately after cutting so that the water is forced up into the hollow stem. After spending years cutting hundreds of cultivated lupine stems, I've also found that turning the stem(s) completely upside down in my hand before plunking helps to send the water straight to the top of the stem.

## POSTHARVEST
Allow the flowers to hydrate and condition for several hours before using, and avoid making a second cut unless you want to do the whole plunking bit all over again. Vase life is three to five days. Can be stored for five days in a cooler.

# *Maianthemum racemosum*
## False Solomon's Seal, Solomon's Plume

The flowers of Solomon's plume light up hillsides in the mountains right around Mother's Day with big fuzzy teardrops of 2- to 4-inch ivory plumes. By late summer, the plumes have transformed into beautiful clusters of brown porcelain berries with red spots. This species forms clumps slowly by underground rhizomes in shaded forests and sometimes open banks.

## USES
The gorgeous flowers are perfect for early season weddings and bouquets for any day. Mix with bright shades of green and any pastels. The berry clusters will hold for a week or two out of water, and bring an abundant touch to arrangements with soft yellows or rich copper and bronze tones.

## HARVEST

Cut flower stems when the first half of the plume is open and slightly fluffy. The berried stems can be cut beginning in late July and until they begin to drop individual berries.

## POSTHARVEST

Flowers can be stored in a 38°F cooler for a week. Vase life is six to eight days. Berries can be dried for use up to a month. Once you've finished using the berries, scatter them in a wooded area with plenty of leaf matter to grow more plants.

# *Monarda* Species

The whorled clusters of monarda flowers, regardless of species, remind me of a bunch of shrimp performing an elaborate synchronized swimming act while singing. The square stems give them away as members of the mint family, and, depending on the species, an herbal scent ranging from sweet to sage-like is evident when you crush the foliage. *Monarda* species make their homes in a wide range of situations and have become specialized into the fine array that

you see here. Every single one is a butterfly magnet, and when butterflies find them, the whole clump moves with their busy wings as they gather the nectar.

## USES

The stem strength and flower size vary by species, but they all make pretty accents in summer arrangements. I love using the white and lavender varieties in pastel compositions—especially bouquets. The pink and red are great mixed with other strong colors like golden yellow rudbeckia, orange lilies, and zinnias. Mix in brilliant blues for a primary-colored theme.

## HARVEST

Cut stems as soon as the first ring of florets appear at the top of the flowering head. They can continue to be cut for a successful vase life through the stage where proceeding rings are right above the halfway point on the head and flower buds are still evident in rings below the open ones.

## POSTHARVEST

Cut stems can be stored in a cooler for up to two weeks, but the foliage will need to be removed. The stiff stems can be easily bent, so handle them lightly. Vase life is four to seven days depending on stage of harvest.

# *Nymphaea odorata*
## Waterlily

Waterlilies live in bodies of still water like lakes, ponds, and swamps. They are most frequently located growing wild in the coastal plain or in the lower altitudes of the rest of the region, although they are hardy enough to survive cold mountain winters. They dig their thick roots way down into the nutritious muck on the bottom of these bodies of water and are often considered a nuisance by landowners. I'll admit, it is frustrating when your fishing line gets tangled up in those pretty lily pads, but it sure has made me improve my casting skills! The flowers are almost otherworldly, so why not take advantage of our native water nymph? An added bonus is the light, lemony scent they exude when fully open.

### USES

The protective outer layer of the flower buds (the calyx) often exhibits warm, rusty tones that beautifully complement the fresh growth of young water oak trees. Mix in airy whites and bright chartreuse colors for chic spring displays. Float waterlilies in a tall, clear vase with some bracken fern spilling out for a splash of cool when the temps heat up.

### HARVEST

Waterlilies can be harvested from a canoe or kayak or along the shore with pole pruners. Wherever you are, look out for snakes. Cut stems underwater up to 18 inches and place immediately in a bucket of water that is as high as the flowers. The timing of waterlily harvesting has a direct impact on both their chance of opening and how long they last once cut. They can be cut in the bud stage when the light pink/white petals are visible and may take two days to open then, or cut the first day they open.

## POSTHARVEST

Native waterlilies are best used as soon as they are harvested. Do not add flower food to the water. If they are harvested in bud stage, they will last about five days, four days for flowers just opened. Many of the flowers will close late in the afternoon and reopen the next morning—just like they do in the pond.

## *Oenothera gaura*

Gaura, Bee Blossom

Gaura is probably most easily recognized as the tough garden perennial with floating white to pink flowers reminiscent of tiny butterflies scattered up and down the sprays of their wiry, waving stalks. There are several species that appear along roadsides from March in the Florida panhandle through August in the high mountains, and each one exudes lighthearted movement.

## USES

Gaura is great as airy filler as long as it is in water. Pair with whites and any pastels or the fruity shades of lilies, dahlias, and zinnias. Some shedding will occur, but the added drama of tiny petals just below the design is the stuff of Dutch still life dreams.

## HARVEST

Cut stems when there is at least one flower open and plenty of unopened buds.

## POSTHARVEST

The individual flowers only last one or two days, but the buds will continue to open along the stem until there are no more. Vase life is directly correlated to how many buds there are on the stem. Gaura stems can hold in a cooler for up to two weeks, but they are far more ethereal when used freshly cut.

# *Phlox* Species

To say the least, phlox flowers are eye catching. Thick mats of moss phlox (*Phlox subulata*) cover sunbaked roadsides and banks beginning as early as February in most southern areas, and the taller varieties continue the show in varying shades of lavender to deep pink (and the occasional white) throughout the growing season. Some even perfume the air with a sweet scent reminiscent of old-fashioned carnations. Whichever species, if phlox is in a happy location, count on it to spread politely.

*Clockwise, from top left: Phlox amplifolia, Phlox carolina, Phlox paniculata, Phlox subulata*

## USES

Moss phlox is tough enough to handle a transplant into a bowl garden for a spring display. All species shed flowers like crazy, but the big flowery heads bring pops of color with a lovely scent that is hard to deny. Add the long stems to any casual wildflower bouquet or arrangement.

## HARVEST

Harvest stems when at least half of the flowers are open, and make sure to strip all of the lower foliage—they will muck up a bucket of water in no time flat.

## POSTHARVEST

When picked at peak, phlox will bloom like crazy and litter your counter for about five days, maybe more. Although they can be held in a cooler for three to four days, the color changes and usually not in a good way.

# *Physostegia virginiana*
## Obedient Plant

Physostegia has earned the common name "obedient plant" because if one gently bends a scape stalk to a desired curve, it will remain in place. This habit has made it a favorable flower among both home and professional flower designers for generations. Obedient plant prefers consistently moist soil and can be found in glades, streambanks, and wet grasslands in varying shades of white to violet depending on the population. Plants spread by roots and can form a large patch given the right conditions, contradicting the well-mannered name.

## USES

The pastel flowering stems of obedient plant lend their spiky form to any arrangement in water or floral foam. What sets them apart from any other spike is that ability to stay put when you bend it. No other spired stem in this book has that ability. Take advantage of that and not just incorporate it as a vertical element, but also use its talents to bring spired, curling movement to compositions.

**HARVEST**
Cut the flowering stems when at least one-quarter to one-third of the flowers have opened.

**POSTHARVEST**
Flowers may be stored cold for a week. Vase life is up to eight days, maybe more depending on the stage that the stem is harvested.

## *Phytolacca americana*
### Pokeweed

Pokeweed is probably my favorite native plant to use in floral design. It can be found on just about any sunny roadside, and I prefer to cut from the plants growing on the most forsaken terrain possible because the foliage is then a brilliant lime green and the stalks and stems are a blazingly bright shade of fuchsia. This statuesque perennial up to 6 feet tall can be a great addition to a large border garden if given the space. Plant judiciously though: You need to remove all of the berries before they drop to the ground or the birds get to them. Otherwise, you may end up with a big patch, and pokeweed has a taproot like a quad-A linebacker has muscles—meaning it will take a big mattock or a jackhammer to remove any mature specimens.

Years ago, I saw it used to great effect above the serpentine walls of the Smithsonian's Ripley Garden. It was late November and cold, but I had somehow stumbled on this gem of a garden at the right time to see a towering pokeweed specimen, still shining with its fuchsia stalks and black berries. It was an "aha" moment in this garden designer's life, and even if it is no longer there, I strongly recommend a visit to that gorgeous garden if you are in the DC area.

Aside from the floral design uses discussed below, the ripe berries are an excellent dye for natural fibers. Although it would take some serious advance planning, how cool would it be to throw a soiree that had tables draped in linens whose color came from the berries and topped with centerpieces loaded with stems from the same species.

## USES
Pokeberry stems can be used as far as your imagination goes. Because of their durability, the stripped stalks can be used as structure in designs that range from small to the truly large—like doorway surrounds and mantelpieces. Flowers and berries can be cut down to any size and added to lower compositions in bowls. When the berries are still green and hard, they can be cut for fresh autumn wreaths and will slowly acquire a purple cast without turning to mush.

## HARVEST
For foliage, flowers, and berries, harvest pokeweed beginning when the entire plant is loaded with about half flowers and half green berries. The bright stalks can be cut from the time they are colored until the first frost.

## POSTHARVEST
Although pokeweed may wilt immediately after it is cut, it is easily rehydrated by cutting the stems underwater and getting them out of the sun. They will drink the water down, so monitor the level. Pokeweed with foliage can go for nine days in water and fourteen days without foliage. Cold storage is not recommended.

# *Polygonatum biflorum*
## Solomon's Seal

Solomon's seal is distinctive in its profile. Once the new growth unwinds from its casing into a clump of vertical stems with the most wonderful downward curve at the top, you can't miss it growing on steep, shaded roadside banks and woods. Simple alternate leaves grow out from about two-thirds of the single stalks at a 90-degree angle and shelter delicate pairs of white flowers tipped in green. The flowers give way to dangling fruits that look like fresh green peas and later change to a deep blue color. The variegated green-and-white foliage of this species' Asian counterparts are highly coveted by both floral designers and gardeners. If I ever encounter a variegated *Polygonatum biflorum*, count on me singing it from the mountaintops. Until then, I am perfectly happy with the green leaves of this versatile 2- to 5-foot-tall plant.

## USES

Solomon's seal brings a unique vertical element to arrangements of any size, and if the foliage is stripped, the flowers and berries add a special touch to bouquets.

## HARVEST

Stems may be cut when the stalks have fully emerged and the white flowers are evident underneath. As always, adhere to the "take less than one-third of any plant" rule here, and if it isn't common in your area, leave it alone.

## POSTHARVEST

Use polygonatum immediately for a vase life of five to six days or store in the cooler for up to ten days. Vase life after storage is four to five days.

# *Pycnanthemum* Species

## Mountain Mint

Multiple species of mountain mint exist in the region and make their appearance along well-drained, sunny to partly shady banks in early to midsummer as flashes of silver against surrounding greenery. When you pick them, the oils from the foliage and stems bring an almost instant cooling sensation to your hands, while the smell refreshes your senses.

## USES

Mountain mint makes a great foliage filler and pairs well with white, lavender, peach, yellow, and green shades. It looks pretty cool against brown too. It does best in water but can tolerate floral foam for a few days as well, so it can definitely be used in large structural installments.

## HARVEST

Cut stems after the lavender florets have bloomed for a week and until it looks shabby.

## POSTHARVEST

Put cut stems into warm water. May be held for four days in a cooler. Vase life is a week.

## *Rudbeckia hirta*
### Black-eyed Susan

Various species of rudbeckia are common roadside flowers throughout the region in sunny, well-drained spots. Unlike their coneflower cousin, echinacea, deer don't like to eat the flowers, and that leaves plenty of them for us to enjoy. Rudbeckia blooms are triggered by long days, but the flowering period often continues in the autumn.

## USES

Rudbeckia is a classic addition to primary-colored wildflower bouquets and also works well with earthier-shaded combinations. The dark seed heads can be used in dried arrangements and wreaths once the petals have dropped.

## HARVEST

The somewhat stiff flowering stems of black-eyed Susans are less susceptible to wilt if they are cut after the pollen appears and when their fresh, shiny centers slowly become more the texture of deep velvet.

**POSTHARVEST**

Use fresh stems immediately. If there is a problem with drooping, they can sometimes be revived by re-cutting into warm water or using a hydrating dip. Do not store in cold—the petals will dull. Vase life is around a week.

## *Sabatia angularis*
### Rose Pink

Sabatia is a charming little biennial that pops up wherever the tiny wind-distributed seeds decide to land. Although it is perfectly happy in a pasture, if it sows itself in a place with more nutrients and water, the resulting plants will be taller. The waxy pink flowers stand out from a distance, and the egg-shaped seedpods are easily distinguished from the aster and goldenrod seed heads that may surround them in December. If you wish to cultivate your own patch, the seeds can be lightly sown in a sunny garden or meadow.

## USES

Sabatia is easily blended into bouquets and arrangements. The cheery pink color adds a visually lightweight pop and looks great with almost any color scheme.

## HARVEST

Since they do not produce a second flush of flowers, stems can be cut as long as plant height allows when about one-third of the flowers are open.

## POSTHARVEST

Rose Pinks have a five- to seven-day vase life. Further testing needs to be done to determine if it is a candidate for cold storage.

# Salvia lyrata

## Lyre Leaf Sage

The pretty blue spires of this salvia rise up from evergreen basal rosettes of slightly puckered foliage that range from green to almost red depending on the population and time of year. The square stems give it away as a member of the mint family. It can form large yet unobtrusive colonies by reseeding in sunny, open areas with loose soils. They flower relatively early—April and May—and then, except for the low foliage, virtually disappear. If you would like to establish your own population, they are easy to start from seed that is either broadcast or germinated and then transplanted.

## USES

Add the bright blue spires to spring mixes—they are a great substitute for delphinium and larkspur.

## HARVEST

Stems can be cut as soon as the first one or two sets of flowers appear at the bottom of the stalk.

## POSTHARVEST

*Salvia lyrata* has a vase life of six to ten days depending on the stage of harvest.

# *Sarracenia flava*
## Yellow Pitcher Plant

The *Sarracenia* genus comprises several species that are unique to North America and predominantly native to the southeastern coastal plain, although a handful of subspecies have adapted to boggy areas of the Appalachian Mountains. By some estimates, this uniquely beautiful group of plants has lost over 95 percent of its natural habitat, so this is another species I am including with a strong caution not to be greedy. Their dwindling populations are too precious to put at risk; unless you find yourself in an area where there are great numbers, leave them alone. If you are lucky enough to have them in plentitude,

only cut a few, and take care not to compact the surrounding earth by trampling it.

## USES

The chartreuse trumpets of pitcher plants are an interesting addition to just about anything. Pair with whites and rosy browns early in the year, and mix with opposite purples late in the season. The old trumpets can be cut in autumn and tucked into wreaths.

## HARVEST

Cut sparingly in any season. If harvesting in spring, wait until the trumpets have filled out and hardened. In autumn, always select the oldest growth.

## POSTHARVEST

Trumpets stay brightly colored in water for about three weeks. They can be dried slowly out of direct light while sitting upright in a container. The color will slowly fade over two to three months.

# *Solidago* Species
## Goldenrod

There are over fifty described species of goldenrod and about as many subspecies. That is a *huge* amount of variety! Goldenrod provides an incredible source of nectar for both common and highly specialized insects at a crucial time of year when days have shortened, there is less available from other plant species, and everybody is fattening up for the winter months to come. The plant itself is also a food source for many Lepidoptera species (butterflies and moths) in the caterpillar stage. Goldenrod lights up just about any area you can think of—including deep, shady forests—with its golden yellow (or infrequently white) inflorescences that present in an array of forms, from single rods to complex panicles. If you ever had the notion that you were allergic to goldenrod, think again. Goldenrod pollen is far too heavy and sticky to be windborne and never makes it far from the plant without the help of pollinating friends. Most allergies that time of year can be blamed on the windborne and ample pollen of green flowering ragweed.

# *Solidago bicolor*

White Goldenrod, Silverrod

# *Solidago curtisii*

Curtis' Goldenrod or Mountain Decumbent Goldenrod

# Solidago odora
Anise-scented Goldenrod

# Solidago gigantea
Giant Goldenrod

## USES

Goldenrod brings a lovely shape to monochromatic compositions of sunflowers, coreopsis, and rudbeckia. It adds sunshine and cascading texture to autumn mixes of rust, peach, and mauve and can also be dried and tucked into seasonal wreaths or dried centerpieces. Goldenrod has long been a staple of brick-and-mortar florists, but they downplay what it actually is by referring to it by its species name—solidago.

## HARVEST

For drying, cut goldenrod before any of the individual buds open. For fresh use, stems may be cut from the time the buds appear and until the flowering heads lose their appeal

## POSTHARVEST

Place cut stems into warm water to hydrate. Depending on species and stage of harvest, vase life is up to fourteen days. Stems may be dried upright in a warm, bright area with good air circulation.

# *Tradescantia virginiana*
## Spiderwort

Spiderwort is common throughout the Southeast and is a reliable source of blue to purple flowers. The individual florets have three petals each and are held in clusters that have a surround of graceful, thin leaflets that flow out and downward, hence the common name. The long, thin stems shoot above waxy bluish-green foliage that brings to mind a clump of upright grass. One of the best things about spiderwort, in my opinion, is *deer won't touch it*, and that says a lot, because if deer are hungry, they will eat a tin can if you spray-paint it green.

## USES

Excellent in any arrangement, it provides an interesting vertical component if stems are left long. Large numbers can be gathered, bunched tightly, and stems cut short to make an unexpected yet classically simple bouquet.

## HARVEST

Harvest after the first flower on the stem has opened.

## POSTHARVEST

If cut in the early stage as recommended, spiderwort will continue to bloom in water for up to fourteen days.

# *Verbena hastata*

## Blue Vervain, Swamp Verbena

The spiky flower inflorescence of this verbena species reminds me of purple fireworks, and they conveniently begin to bloom around the Fourth of July. Colonies of this short-lived perennial can be found growing in sunny ditches, and some of the larger specimens can reach 5 feet tall along sunny riverbanks. There are quite a few escapees in the *Verbena* genus that have migrated from their more southern homes and established themselves along road-sides in the region, and most of those differ from *Verbena hastata* in that they prefer very dry growing conditions. The seeds of most can be collected in late summer and broadcast through a natural garden setting for germination and bloom the following season.

## USES

The tiny florets set on the lightly spired inflorescences bring a similar but more delicate texture than lavender in bouquets and centerpiece arrangements.

## HARVEST

Begin cutting stems when the first tiny flowers appear. The stalk will branch and produce more stems if cut at this early stage.

## POSTHARVEST

Best if used fresh but can be stored in a cooler for up to two weeks. Vase life is a week with a bit of shedding.

# *Vernonia* Species
## Ironweed

Ironweed species are late season bloomers with umbels of royal-purple flowers topping plants that range from 2 to 8 feet tall, depending on the species. Giant ironweed towers above just about everything in neglected pastures of Appalachia and the Piedmont, and appear just before their seasonal companions, goldenrod, begin to really show off. In some years, depending on the weather, they are both in full swing at the same time, like a pasture full of New

Orleans Saints fans. Other ironweed species of the Piedmont and coastal plain aren't as tall and have narrower leaves. Although they are less visible in the landscape, they are just as tough as their metallic common name insinuates.

## USES

Even before the flowers begin to open, the nearly black flower stems can be cut long and used whole as a textural component in large installations, or trimmed down to add some dark drama to boutonnieres. The purple flowers are best paired with other saturated colors, from yellow to red and the richer shades of pink and coral. They add depth to native combinations of minty green foliage and starry blue asters. Some species can be dried, but more experimentation needs to be done.

## HARVEST

Cut stems when the heads are fully formed and the highest buds show just a bit of purple fuzz at the tips. This is the best time to harvest for drying. For fresh use, cut as long as they are presentable. Once the heads form seeds, there will be shedding.

## POSTHARVEST

For fresh use, stems can be held in cold storage for up to three weeks. Vase life is up to ten days. For dried stems, place upright in a container and allow to dry in a covered yet open area that has good air circulation.

## *Zephranthes atamasca*
Atamasco Lily

Large colonies of Atamasco lilies can be seen blooming in late March through early April in low-lying areas and disappear as the trees leaf out above and the foliage of their various small neighbors grow up and surround them.

The delicacy of their light pink buds and glistening white flowers belie their toughness, and they perennially return from ever-multiplying bulbs. My great-aunt Virginia had her gardener dig a few up from roadsides each spring for years and replant them, gradually creating a collection that numbered in the hundreds. They carpeted the lawn that rolled from the longleaf pine–shaded white house down to the pond where a pair of white swans swam in their lithesome way. That spectacular display, culminating with their blooms' peak around Easter time, is a childhood memory that certainly helped define my love of flowers today.

## USES

A handful of Atamasco lilies displayed in a vase is a simply perfect centerpiece for any spring gathering. They are also quite lovely mixed with fresh greenery and any pastel bloom of the season.

## HARVEST

Cut stems at the base when they are in bud, leaving the surrounding foliage to feed the bulbs. Like other lilies, cutting Atamasco lilies while in bud prevents the bruising and breakage that may occur when the flowers are fully open.

**POSTHARVEST**

Use immediately, and pay attention to the vase water level—these lilies are thirsty and will drink it up quickly. Flowers cut in bud will last five to seven days.

# *Zizia aurea*

## Golden Alexander

Golden alexander is found on the shaded rocky banks of the mountains early in the growing season. It reminds me of a yellow Queen Anne's lace or small heads of flowering dill, but the stems holding the 4-inch umbels are less stiff and therefore have a sweet bounciness to them. Golden alexander is not to be confused with introduced wild parsnip, which occurs in the same mountainous areas but blooms later, thrives in sun, grows four times taller, and whose sap is phototoxic.

## USES

I love adding a bit of golden alexander to anything I can in the early flowering months. It is a lovely contrast to pointy baptisia flowers and brings a bit of sunshine to the soft pink bunches of foraged dame's rocket (*Hesperis matronalis*).

## HARVEST

Flowers can be cut as soon as their yellow glow is evident and until it fades.

## POSTHARVEST

Use golden alexander immediately or hold for a week in cold storage.

# VINES

VINES ARE PLANTS THAT NEED SUPPORT AND CLIMB. The word is derived from the Latin-based *vinea*, which refers to vine, vineyard, and wine. These climbers may be annual, perennial, or woody, and since they all perform a similar task in floral design, they are grouped together here.

The cool thing about these plants is that each species has evolved its own method of climbing whatever support they manage to be near. Some vines wrap themselves around anything they touch with the primary growing stems. Others have adapted thorns that point downward and anchor the stems as they head toward the sky. Leaves are designed to wrap themselves around whatever they touch, and tendrils are modified hair-like leaves that cling to a surface with either sticky, rounded tips or a tiny claw at the tip. Other tendrils simply wave themselves around until they touch something and then curl like a hungry python around its prey. There even are vines that might incorporate one of these mechanisms in their juvenile stage, send out roots along the stem as they go up, and when they are satisfied with the conditions, morph into their adult stage with completely different-looking leaves and begin to flower—think creeping fig, poison ivy, and English ivy as examples. Whatever the means, these plants will go to great lengths to reach the sun, which they need to make food through photosynthesis.

From a design standpoint, vines are a valuable addition to any florist's tool kit because they easily express movement when thoughtfully placed. The biggest vines can be wrapped into a circular base of a wreath and into baskets for vessels that hold, well, anything. Less obtrusive species with attractive flowers, foliage, or berries can bring an unexpected flair to arrangements. Native species send a uniquely trailing sense of place.

## *Apios americana*
Potato Vine, Groundnut

This gorgeous perennial vine is a member of the legume family and climbs by wrapping its stems loosely around its supportive neighbors. The common names refer to the small, edible tubers that form underground chains next to rivers, creeks, and hammocks throughout the region. The small brown flowers

appear in late summer and recall those of its cousin, wisteria, but they are far more polite and much more interesting, in my opinion.

### USES
This elegant vine is perfect to hang down from the rim of tall vases and is lightweight enough to gently twist upward onto any vertical branches in a design mimicking its natural habit.

### HARVEST
The flowers come and go within a two-week window, so harvest when you see them. The stems are more delicate than those on a woody vine, so be gentle. Begin at the growing tip, work your way back, and then cut.

### POSTHARVEST
Use immediately and expect a vase life of one week.

# *Aristolochia macrophylla*

## Jack Vine, Pipevine

This woody vine is an impressive climber, sometimes growing over 30 feet on the woody slopes and ravines of the Blue Ridge Mountains, where it is locally known as jack vine. The more often used name, pipevine, refers to the shape of the single flowers. The plant is the exclusive diet of the pipevine swallowtail butterfly larvae, which feasts on its large, heart-shaped leaves.

### USES
Use jack vine foliage as a grounding base in arrangements with spiky and airy flowers. The thick, woody vines are quite flexible and can be wrapped into large wreath forms and even baskets big and strong enough to hold a person.

### HARVEST
Harvest the new growth of the vine for foliage once it has hardened off. Choose stems that do not have fruit or flowers. The woody vines can be cut any time.

### POSTHARVEST
Use foliage immediately for a vase life of one week. Woody vines need to be formed into their desired shape right after harvest, before they dry and lose their flexibility.

# *Bignonia capreolata*
## Crossvine

Crossvine is a spring-blooming cousin of trumpet vine whose muted red and golden orange flowers smell like hot chocolate (seriously!). The foliage is semi-evergreen and turns burgundy when temperatures drop in early winter. I always catch glimpses of its blooms running up the sides of trees along the interstate in April, and there is a very noticeable patch growing on a chain link fence around Macon, Georgia, in what I consider just about the worst growing conditions around—between two highways in poor, sun-baked soil. This woody vine is a great addition to gardens if given a structure, like an arch or pergola, to climb, and the foliage will persist through the winter.

## USES
Crossvine makes a colorful, surprising addition to designs in need of a cascading element, such as wedding bouquets and large centerpieces. Shorter stems can be tucked into little arrangements.

## HARVEST
Cut stems as long as needed—1 to 3 feet long—with flowers and foliage, when one-third of the flowers are open and immediately place in water. If the outside temperature is under 75°F, harvest any time of day. If over that, wait until it cools off before you cut.

## POSTHARVEST
Once harvested, the lower 6 inches of the stem can be stripped, the end recut, and placed in warm to hot water and allowed to cool. Vase life is around five days—depending on how many unopened flowers are on the stem.

# *Campsis radicans*
## Trumpet Vine

Trumpet vine climbs with tendrils and is a common sight covering fences and telephone poles along roadsides throughout the region. The bright orange trumpet, or tubular-shaped, flowers that begin in May and continue through

August jump out from the landscape, especially in the lull of hot July, after many of the early summer flowers have finished blooming and the late season blooms are not quite ready to show themselves. If you are considering this woody vine for the garden, choose the spot carefully. Trumpet vines need something at least 10 feet tall to climb and full sun to bloom, and once it takes off, good luck getting rid of it. It sends up suckers from the roots wherever they are disturbed, and even if you pull up the parent plant, those suckers may continue to emerge for another fifteen years. That said, its showy flowers are a hummingbird magnet.

## USES

Trumpet vine is an excellent cut flower—both the showy flowers and the compound pinnate foliage bring color, texture, and movement to any type of large arrangement. I like pairing them with Turk's cap lilies in the mountains and butterfly milkweed, liatris, and yarrow in the lowlands.

## HARVEST

Cut the flowering tips of vines as the first flower in a cluster opens. Stems can be up to 2.5 feet long.

## POSTHARVEST

Put split and cut stems into warm water and you will enjoy the blooms for up to a week.

# *Clematis virginiana*
## Virgin's Bower, Traveler's Joy

This vigorous native clematis climbs with specialized leaves whose stalks twist around other vegetation or support. Woodbine is a member of the buttercup family (Ranunculaceae) and has abundant white flowers on panicles that begin to appear in August. It is not to be confused with its introduced Asian cousin, *Clematis terniflora*, which blooms later with slightly larger flowers and more leathery leaves. The seed heads for after flowering explain its other common names—"devil's darning needles" and "devil's hair." Don't worry, though, there is nothing devilish about these hairy fruits that resemble tiny air plants, and they are just as useful as the flowers for arrangements.

### USES

Clematis is good for trailing out and down large arrangements, bouquets, and arbor pieces. The flowering stems can be cut short and tucked into smaller designs to bring lightness to heavier blooms. Once seeded, they are perfect for bringing texture to autumn arrangements.

## HARVEST

After cutting hundreds of these vine stems for florists, I've learned to stay very organized through the process in order not to end up with a tangled, useless mess. When you find a patch that you want to cut from, have everything ready before you begin—rubber bands, clippers, pole pruners, and water buckets filled halfway—because this is something you only want to do once. Find the growing tip of a stem and work your way back 14 to 36 inches. Carefully unwrap any leaves that have wound around something else and then cut. After you have cut five to seven stems the same length, rubber band them together at the base and place in the water bucket. Do not crowd the bunches in the bucket. If you need longer pieces, don't bunch them, and once you've finished, make sure they are spread out from the bucket, so they stay pretty.

Cut flowering stems as the first buds begin to open; cut seeded stems as soon as they look hairy. The seed heads change from hairy to fuzzy and hairy in a few days and then they begin to float away—plan accordingly.

## POSTHARVEST

Cut stems with flowers or seeds can hold in a cooler for a week before use and have a vase life of five days each. It is worth experimenting with drying the seed heads to see if there is a harvest window where they stay hairy.

## *Dioscorea villosa*
### Wild Yam Vine

Wild yam vine is an attractive perennial vine that spreads via underground rhizomes and climbs with twisting stems in various degrees of politeness depending on their location. The shiny, heart-shaped leaves have around eleven veins that originate from a central point at the base. Although the flowers are barely noticeable, the winged green fruits are held in interesting clusters.

## USES

Use the foliage stems of wild yam, with or without seeds, as a trailing element, or gently twist it upward to mimic its natural growth in any large arrangement.

## HARVEST

Harvest after vines have emerged and the foliage has hardened off enough that it doesn't wilt immediately after being cut.

## POSTHARVEST

Vase life is ten days. Can be stored in a cooler for a week.

# *Gelsimium sempervirens*
## Carolina Jessamine

Carolina jessamine is a woody vine with a habit of scrambling up anything with its thin, winding stems—be it pine tree or fence—and shouting from its yellow trumpet-shaped flowers that spring has truly arrived. It can be seen festooned and glowing along roadsides and into pine forests through March and April. Do not confuse it with invasive Japanese honeysuckle, which has smaller, lighter-colored flowers that bloom later. Carolina jessamine is *not* edible like honeysuckle is, so save it for decoration.

## USES

The flowers are usually blooming around the same time as dogwood and both late tulips and daffodils, and give movement to spring compositions. The attractive green foliage can be cut any time to add vining movement as well.

## HARVEST

Cut flowering vines with pole pruners when the flowers are open. If you don't have pole pruners, find some growing on a fence line—it's everywhere.

## POSTHARVEST

Use immediately for a vase life of up to ten days.

# *Lonicera sempervirens*
## Flame or Trumpet Honeysuckle

Although I've always known about this woody vine, the first time I saw it blooming in the wild, just west of Mexico Beach, Florida, I nearly drove off the road! I was on the hunt for some cool panhandle natives to play with while at my family's beach place and couldn't believe my luck when the coral-red flower corymbs caught my eye as they clung to a yaupon (*Ilex vomitoria*). Hurricane Michael leveled Mexico Beach in October 2018, and my fingers are crossed that both the town and its surrounding natural coastal plain beauty will rebound. Unlike its aggressive and invasive cousin, Japanese honeysuckle, *Lonicera sempervirens* politely climbs surrounding brush by winding itself around branches and stems. I love the way its oppositely set foliage is fused together to form an oval cup just below the flowers.

## USES
Use the curling woody stems of flame honeysuckle to bring movement to any design. The hanging clusters of honeysuckle flowers can be placed as the stems trail either horizontally or twirl upward out of a vase. Mix with other reds, oranges, and whites that are around when they are.

## HARVEST
Cut honeysuckle stems with pole pruners when the flowers are bright and visible.

## POSTHARVEST
Blooming honeysuckle has a vase life of five to ten days, depending on harvest stage. Use it when you get it.

# *Nekemias arborea*
## Pepper Vine

Pepper vine is a member of the woody grapevine family. The bipinnate, shiny lime-green foliage is accentuated by red stems and tendrils. Attractive clusters of pale green flowers give way to porcelain pink, blue, and purple berries. On an explorative trip to one of Charleston's barrier islands in early July, I was disheartened by the lack of interesting cuttable stems all the way down there. I had left flower Valhalla in the mountains, and the only colorful thing I could see for one hundred miles going eighty miles per hour along the I-26 corridor was trumpet vine. (By the way, I *can* differentiate between long-leaf, loblolly, and slash pines at that speed.) Been there, done that. The pink mimosa flowers had already fried themselves in the heat, and aside from an occasional magnolia bloom, most natives were obviously on vacation.

Then I took a stroll to the beach. Beach access on Sullivan's Island is by paths that are situated every block or so along the length of the island. This barrier island has built itself up gradually, and the area between the sea oat–covered dunes and the green lawns of beach homes has filled in with a protective tangle of waxmyrtle, cat briar (*Smilax* spp.), and this lovely vine. Honestly, I'd never noticed it before, and peering closely at the berries, all I could think was "Well hello there, who are you?" I took some photos, then cut a few pieces and hauled them back home to the mountains. For good measure, I left them in the bucket on our gravel courtyard in full blazing sun for a week. They never lost their luster. This is a strong-growing vine, and to those of you that may deal with it as a pest, all I can say is—better than kudzu or poison ivy! This one, like pokeweed, is a free-for-all.

## USES
Pepper vine can give movement and lacy-foliaged elegance to large installments such as arbors, and can be cut down to fit smaller centerpieces. This is an excellent choice for those living along the coast, and although it will drop foliage in a hard freeze, its yellowed foliage can bring autumn color to designs in an area that sees little change during the colder months.

## HARVEST
Harvest stems up to 6 feet until the foliage drops. Pole pruners may be helpful but are not necessary—the vine is strong enough to pull away from whatever it is growing on without breaking it. Watch out for poison ivy that may grow close to it.

## POSTHARVEST
Place cut stems in warm water and store in the shade. Cold storage is not recommended. Vase life is up to fourteen days. If you are using stems with berries, remove those that have turned a glossy dark purple to prevent them from staining anything.

# *Parthenocissus quinquefolia*
## Virginia Creeper

This common woody vine is a member of the grape family, although neither the fruits nor the lustrous green foliage are edible. Virginia creeper is easily distinguished from its evil cousin, poison ivy, by the number of leaflets: Its palmately compound leaflets are in groups of five as opposed to poison ivy's three. Virginia creeper uses specially adapted tendrils with very cool adhesive tips that help them attach to surfaces—like minute droplets of Post-It Note glue that turn into Portland cement. In a garden setting, this polite scramble makes it a better choice than English Ivy (*Hedera helix*) or creeping fig (*Ficus pumila*), which attach themselves to structures with damaging roots. A bonus is the spectacular color display every autumn.

## USES
Virginia creeper can be used any time during the growing season, but it really shines from early to late fall when the berries have turned a lovely matte

bluish-gray to navy and the foliage starts to change colors. Give large arrangements, centerpieces, and large installations colorful movement by letting lengths of it cascade out of tall vases. In lower vessels, position the vine so that it trails across the surface where it is displayed, lending a beautiful horizontality to the design. Pair with sky-blue and white aster species, goldenrod, pale blushing dahlias, and any white flowers blooming in your garden. Any warm autumn tone blends well with Virginia creeper as well.

## HARVEST

Harvest the growing ends for the most delicate effect. Pole pruners work best for this tall vine unless you find some closer to the ground. This is a vine with presence, so if you are only doing one arrangement, seek out no more than five perfect pieces. Cut the length needed and then pull it up and away from whatever it is growing on. Take care when pulling it off a tree—the more tender tips may break in an unreachable spot if you pull in the wrong way or too briskly.

## POSTHARVEST

Use immediately; there is always plenty more out there. Vase life for the foliage is seven days in water, four days in floral foam. Berry life depends on stage of harvest, but let's say a week. Although the berries will not stay plump for long out of water after being cut, they may retain their color for up to ten days.

# *Passiflora incarnata*

## Maypop, Passionflower

Passionflowers possess some of the most complex looking and beautifully showy flowers I have ever seen. There are a couple of *Passiflora* species that occur in the Southeast, but the most noticeable is the maypop. These lavender- and purple-flowered beauties are apparently nicknamed for the sound they make when you throw the rounded, slightly oblong fruits at an unsuspecting sibling or neighborhood friends. It can be found thriving along baking roadsides, in the middle of horse-grazed pastures, and on bald banks behind supermarkets—all in sandy, well-drained soil.

### USES

Passionflowers and fruits lend an exotic touch to arrangements, and the vines create a sense of movement as they flow out of vases and cascade down hanging installations. Individual flowers last only one day, beginning with the buds closest to the base of the vine and working their way to the sky. If you want to use them singly—in a boutonniere, for example—you will need to figure out their timing in advance. The yellowish fruits are an excellent visual *pop* (pun intended) in autumn arrangements.

### HARVEST

Cut passionflower vines when the first flower or two has opened. Shorter pieces—12 to 24 inches—work best.

### POSTHARVEST

Use immediately. Vase life depends on how many unopened buds are on the cut vine. One flower will stay open a day or two and then another one opens.

# *Smilax* Species

## Greenbriar

There are quite a few species of *Smilax* throughout the region. Some species spread slowly via underground rhizomes and can form nearly impenetrable thickets along fence lines, while other types climb trees, hang down, and show off their fabulous stem arrangement. Although coarse at times, this plant brings the Fibonacci sequence, or golden ratio, to life at the most basic and subliminal way possible. You don't know why you like it, but it just makes sense. One of my favorite species is *Smilax smallii*, also known as Jackson vine or just plain "smilax." This evergreen version is popular among both florists and home gardeners. It is elegant and easy to handle, yet tough. It doesn't wilt for days after it is cut, and doesn't get away from you when it's trained over an arbor or the arch of a front door. When I was in my twenties, I worked for a garden designer in Raleigh. I remember the remark that just about every past and present member of the Raleigh Junior League had smilax growing over their front entrance. This came from a sustaining member with a beautiful garden who knew exactly what she was talking about.

As for the other species out there, choose them according to your needs. Deciduous species have clusters of waxy navy-blue berries that persist through even the coldest winter. The

new growth is edible, with a light asparagus flavor, and is prized by innovative chefs.

## USES

Evergreen smilax is suited to large-scale installations in need of a strong green background. Drape the long pieces over doors and mantels for the holidays and secure by wiring them to small nails. I love using the deciduous types in wreaths beginning in the fall and going through winter after the foliage has dropped or been removed. The berried green stems can be left as is or given a light coat of plant-friendly metallic spray paint to accent their structure. Once the new growth has hardened off, these varieties are also great hanging from arbors.

## HARVEST

Harvest stems any time of year. Jackson vine doesn't have thorns, but it is tall and pole pruners are recommended. The thorns on the other species aren't all mean, but leather gloves are never a bad idea.

## POSTHARVEST

During cool months, coils of evergreen smilax can be stored temporarily on the shady side of a building on moist but not wet ground as long as temps remain above freezing. They will look good for three to four weeks as outside decorations. If drying and gilding, lay vines in a straight line in a dry, warm spot for a week or two before blinging them out. Vines without foliage can be sprayed immediately. They will last indefinitely if protected from excess moisture.

# *Vitis*

Grapevine, Muscadine

# *Vitis labrusca*
Fox Grape

Finally, in this group of climbing plants are grapes, the plants that give vines their name. From the mountains to the sea, tangles of native grapes can be found climbing trees with their tendrils. As the looping, swinging, hanging woody vines get big with age in the shady understory, they create natural

playgrounds where a child's imagination is the only limit. In the sunshine above the canopy, they produce berries for juice, jelly, and wine. Scrappy muscadines of the coastal plain and Piedmont are more adapted to heat and drought: Their leaves are smaller, the big berries have a thick-textured skin that is often green or bronze and are arranged in groups of three or four, and they are nearly impervious to disease. Fox grapes, their musky-scented mountain cousins, display their classic grape-looking clusters of smooth purple berries below deep green foliage.

## USES

In spring the fresh leafy growth of grapes makes a good backdrop to any arrangement—I seek out pieces with off-colored foliage to highlight what-ever I am working on. Berried stems can grace temporary large installations in autumn and convey the abundance of the season. Pair with deep purple, white, ivory, and copper shades for a sophisticated compilation. The colorful fall foliage is just as wonderful for autumnal displays. The woody vines can be wound into wreath frames and baskets any time of year—especially if you have a thicket that needs taming.

## HARVEST

Grape foliage is hard to hydrate in the summer months and is best left to grow while there are plenty of other vining options then. Cut both fresh and fall stems with pole pruners to a desired length. Woody vines can be cut any time—just be prepared to shape them immediately. If you want to make a bunch of wreath frames, be ready to do so when you cut them.

## POSTHARVEST

Place cut and split stems with foliage or fruits into warm water. Vase life for spring foliage is seven to ten days. The vase life for berried stems is five days. Storage for these is not recommended.

# WOODY SHRUBS AND TREES

WOODIES ARE A BIG GROUP OF PLANTS that come in many forms. The physical characteristic that defines them all is their woody tissue, which covers and supports the primary stems, roots, and branches. There are evergreens with needles and those with broadleaf foliage. Deciduous woodies (meaning they drop all their leaves when entering the dormant phase) are usually broadleaved types, but there are needled species that drop all their foliage as well. Some shoot straight to the sky and some creep along the ground, while others are content somewhere in between. Woody plants can be enduring—the oldest single living organism on Earth, a five-thousand-year-old bristlecone pine in California, was no longer a youngster when the Egyptians built the great pyramids. They can be huge—a clonal grove of aspen sharing the same set of roots in Utah, known as Pando, is one of the most massive living organisms known. On the other end of the spectrum, tiny willow and beech "trees" creep along in the Arctic and never reach more than 1 inch in height. Woody plants absorb $CO_2$, release the oxygen we breathe into the air, hold the earth in place with their spreading roots, and shade us from the sun. If not for these plants, we would suffocate and bake on the stony earth.

Woody shrubs and trees are also beautiful in their diversity and lend their foliaged, flowering, fruiting branches to us, only asking that we exhale in return.

## *Acer* Species
### Maples

The list of maple species endemic to the Southeast is somewhat short. They all have lobed leaves arranged oppositely on the stems, but when maple trees come to mind, the physical characteristics of red maples are likely the ones most recalled. Both the straight species—*Acer rubrum*—and various subspecies are widely distributed throughout the region. Southern sugar maples—*Acer floridanum*—grow in the coastal plain and Piedmont, while the northern sugar maples are more likely to thrive in the cooler mountains.

The most unusual one, the green stripe maple, named for the vertical stripes on the bark of younger plants, grows rather exclusively in the Appalachian Mountains. Colonies of this little maple are found in the forest understory, and it has more-rounded yet still lobed foliage that changes from a light green

*Acer pensylvanicum*

*Acer rubrum*

to pure yellow in the autumn. Another distinguishing feature of this species is the abundance of large, light green clusters of winged fruit that hang onto the branches well into late summer. When I cut branches of them and strip the foliage, even the most seasoned of florists erupt in glee when they see them, with a curious "what is that?" look in their eyes.

## USES

Regardless of where you live, what species you choose, or when you need them, maple trees provide three seasons of beautiful material. With their salmon- to brick-colored glow, maple flower buds are a sure sign of spring. They begin to erupt about the time daffodils are blooming, and from those richly shaded flowers come the hanging clusters of the winged fruit. Catch them at the right time and you will be rewarded with ample branches of subtle texture and color that will even evolve from one stage to the next in a large vase within a week or two.

*Acer saccharum*

## HARVEST

Harvest maples when you need them—from flower bud stage to full-blown autumn leaf coloration. Branches may be cut from 1 to 4 feet.

## POSTHARVEST

Place split and cut stems into warm water. If you are cutting in the bud stage and want a long display, pay attention to the water level.

# *Aralia spinosa*
## Devil's Walking Stick

This woody species of aralia strikes a unique silhouette along the forest's edge with its thorny, thin, leggy trunks that are topped with huge (up to 4 feet) compound bipinnate leaves. The large panicles of white flowers glow when they are in bud and gradually transition to clusters of shining black berries on bright pink stems that hang with juicy weight when mature. Like its perennial cousin, *Aralia racemosa* (American spikenard), which thrives in the mountains and farther north, the berries drop quickly and although tempting to use will likely result in a big mess. The flower panicles, however, are quite spectacular in their 1- to 4-foot size and strong open form. In combination with the foli-

age and flowers, the aralia's sculptured architecture is like a giant vase of flowers in the landscape and would make a great addition to a large garden. I would love to see a specimen growing out of a giant pot or several grouped in a raised bed—with either combination giving a nod to the fantastical plants seen in Dr. Seuss books.

## USES

The tall flowering stems are perfect for vase arrangements of epic proportions and can also be used in free-standing installations. The flower clusters can be cut down and tucked into lower coordinating table centerpieces and even bouquets and boutonnieres. Pair with tall flowering perennials of the season, like Joe pye weed, and add branches of ninebark, cotinus, or cornus cultivars with chartreuse foliage.

**HARVEST**

Cut stems when flowers are in bud. A shorter set of pole pruners may be needed. Take care to avoid the thorny woody part of the stalks or wear leather gloves—they don't call it devil's walking stick for nothing!

**POSTHARVEST**

Put split stems into warm water. If the flowers are cut in bud, vase life is two weeks.

# *Callicarpa americana*
## Beautyberry

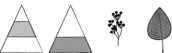

Beautyberry can be found across the lower altitudes of the Southeast but are most abundant in the coastal plain. Its whorled clusters of electric purple berries going all the way up the stems look like little else outside of the genus and are some of the most beautiful found in nature. They flower on new growth and therefore benefit from a hard cutting every autumn. This is an excellent landscape plant and easy to cultivate unless you are in high mountains, where substituting with the hardier Japanese species, *Calllicarpa dichotoma*, is recommended.

Seek out the white-berried cultivars of either species and you will be rewarded with an abundance of berried stems that are an ideal substitute for both the invasive tallow tree and the difficult-to-grow-here snowberry.

## USES

Beautyberry can stand alone and is also a brilliant counter to the oranges, reds, and yellows of the season. Mix those colors and set them against a background of deep burgundy foliage, or balance that purple with cool, minty green foliage and silver. Large arrangements, bouquets, fresh wreaths, and fascinator/arbor pieces are all great ways to use beautyberry.

## HARVEST

Stems perform best if they are cut, split, and *immediately* placed in a bucket of hot water. Harvest when most of the berries have colored up. Don't wait until after a frost or when the lower clusters begin to drop.

## POSTHARVEST

If you didn't already, split and place stems in hot water with flower food. Store in a cool, dark, humid place for a couple of days and then strip the foliage, because it doesn't last. When harvested at the early stage recommended, they will stay pretty in water for up to two weeks. I've experimented with drying this species for wreath use, and although the dried berries are nothing like the glorious fresh ones, the purple color is retained for some time, albeit in a shriveled state.

# *Calycanthus floridus*

Carolina Allspice, Sweet Shrub, Bubby Bush

Carolina allspice is a rounded deciduous shrub that grows up to about 10 feet and can be found in suckering colonies along creeks, rivers, and moist woodlands scattered throughout the Southeast. The strappy-petaled flowers of this member of the laurel family are a deep burgundy red, and the buds appear on straight, woody stems just before the foliage in spring and continue to fill out and open as the plant covers itself in opposite, glossy, ovate foliage. Although there are many common names for this species, it became endeared to me as "Bubby Bush" when I heard it referred to as such by my neighbors. This southern Appalachian colloquialism is a reference to where ingenious ladies placed the fragrant blossoms on hot days—mostly before they went to church—long before air conditioning. They tucked them between and under their "bubbies" so the sweet smell could emanate up and out of their dresses, thus masking any unwanted odors that might occur in sweaty, close situations. I say, "Use what you have and bless your hearts for it, folks!"

## USES

Not just the scent, but the uncommon color and flower form make this a wonderful addition to spring designs. Mix with any type of baptisia, mock orange, and both false and true Solomon's seal for rich and interesting native compositions. Allow the entire mix to verge on statuesque as long stems, or cut shorter,

multiflowered pieces to tuck into otherwise loose, garden-style arrangements. I love weaving them into corsages, boutonnieres, and bouquets.

## HARVEST

Flowering stems can be harvested as soon as the flowers buds are full and visible, and can continue through their fully open stage when all of the petals have peeled away from the center. The later the harvest stage, the better the smell.

## POSTHARVEST

Place cut and split the woody stems into warm water. Stems harvested in the earlier stages of flowering will last up to ten to fourteen days, and seven days when they are more open. They can be stored between 38–42°F for a week.

# *Cercis canadensis*

Eastern Redbud

Flowering redbuds are a quintessential sign of spring throughout the South. Around the same time that *Cornus florida* is blooming white, this small tree explodes with purplish-pink flowers borne directly on the branches. Its clusters of beanlike seedpods give it away as a member of the legume family. Redbuds will grow just about anywhere but have more flowers in full sun.

## USES

Redbud branches can be used in large, single-species arrangements or mixed with seasonal native companions such as dogwood, Carolina jessamine, crabapple, and maple, as well as cultivated daffodils, tulips, and Japanese magnolia varieties.

## HARVEST
Cut branches up to 3 feet long when the buds are full and beginning to open. Stems can be forced out of season, but I haven't tried it.

## POSTHARVEST
Store at 40°F for up to a week. Vase life is about a week.

## *Chionanthus virginicus*

Fringetree, Greybeard

Greybeard is a small deciduous tree with white flowers in spring that hang down in an open ball of snowy fringe. When the bloom disappears, the tree melts into the green backdrop of the shady understory that it prefers and is forgotten until it lights up again the following year. This 15- to 30-foot-tall, slow-to-emerge species is naturally found throughout the region in moist woodlands. I also notice it solitarily placed in the yards of about 20 percent of the country houses I pass in the spring. This is a beloved, old-fashioned plant, and I imagine Southern ladies of the past putting on their gardening clothes and going out to the woods to get one they saw for their garden—or convincing their husbands to do so on a casual "Honey Do" list.

## USES

Greybeard adds pure white lightness to any arrangement. Flowering branches can be cut longer and set as a cloudlike filler above other stems, or cut short and placed at the base of a vase with heavier selections. It blooms when Pinxter azaleas, Atamasco lilies, Cherokee roses, itea, gopherweed, and some species of blackberries do and looks fetching with them all. Try it hanging from a bride's bouquet—either go all white, pop in some pinks, or add yellows and oranges.

## HARVEST

Harvest when the flowers are evident. I haven't experimented as much with this one, but like most woody plants, the sooner the better to harvest for flexibility and shed prevention.

## POSTHARVEST

Earlier cuts will likely endure in a vase for up to six days. Later cuts are more like three days. Worth testing in cold storage.

# *Cornus* Species

Dogwoods

Although most of us equate the name dogwood tree with our large-bracted *Cornus florida*, which possesses the story of Easter in its ivory flowers, there are a couple of other species sprinkled around the region that bring ornamental delight to those of us on the hunt for interesting design elements four seasons out of the year.

# *Cornus alternifolia*

Pagoda Dogwood, Alternate Leaf Dogwood

Pagoda dogwoods are small trees with alternate foliage that is somewhat whorled at the ends of the attractively divided branches and topped with rounded umbels of creamy white flowers in spring. The branches of this species grow from the trunk in a rather horizontal manner until the ends, where they curve upward. The entire framework of the tree has been compared to the Asian architecture that gives it its common name.

## USES
When cut long, the fanned yellow branches of pagoda dogwoods give a definitive outline to large spring arrangements, with or without flowers.

## HARVEST
Harvest branches with ideal shape and size when they become evident in spring. That is the best time to harvest, because after the flowers fade, the trees disappear into the green sea of summer foliage. I like to cut these when it is raining to keep them happy, and it usually involves pole pruners.

## POSTHARVEST
Stems can be stored cold for a week or two. Vase life is six to seven days.

# *Cornus ammomum*

## Silky Dogwood

Silky dogwoods are large shrubs that spread by suckers in moist, low areas. I love this species for two reasons: the clusters of porcelain blue berries that become visible in late August, and the flexible straight stems that turn a rich maroon red when temperatures drop in December.

## USES

Use the berried branches in late summer arrangements with warm pastel flowers and rosy brown foliage. A few of the thin red stems can be trained and wired onto a round metal frame for a modern-looking wreath, or short tip pieces can be tucked in clusters onto traditional evergreen wreaths. They are also a great vertical component in winter vase arrangements.

## HARVEST

Harvest the berried branches when they are transitioning from green to blue. Cut the red stems when the foliage falls, and they can be seen glowing from a distance.

## POSTHARVEST

Berried stems should be cut short, split, and hydrated constantly—vase life is five days. They may be a candidate for temporary dried use, but that needs more experimentation. The red stems don't need any processing and will look good out of water for a winter month or two. Stems in water may eventually send out roots and foliage if in the right conditions.

# *Cornus florida*

Flowering Dogwood

This dogwood in flower is our classic symbol of a Southern spring and hardly needs an introduction. The species has had a hard time fighting fungus over the last thirty years, but wild populations still light up both forest understory and roadsides beginning in March.

## USES

Use flowering dogwood branches as tall framework in large arrangements, or cut them down for low centerpieces. Depending on the branches you select, they can even be worked in as horizontal elements.

## HARVEST

For the best vase life, harvest stems when the creamy flower bracts are still small and tight. It is also possible to force the blooms open by cutting stems when the buds are swollen in late winter and bringing them into a warm room.

## POSTHARVEST

The hard wood of dogwood stems needs to be split immediately and placed in hot water. When harvested in the early stage of bloom, stems can be held in a cooler for up to two weeks. Once they come out of storage, cut the stems again and place in warm water. Vase life is seven to ten days.

# *Corylus americana*
## Wild Hazelnut

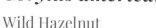      

American filberts are large, suckering shrubs that are most easily spotted along wooded roadsides in February and March when their long yellow catkins are blooming. They are just about the only shrub of that size with any color when they first show themselves. The parrot-like, pale green husks that hang below the attractive foliage hold edible nuts that ripen in September.

## USES

The early season blooms are great for single-branch arrangements. Branches are good to use for both the foliage and the husks, to add texture to arrangements of any kind. Once the husks have browned and dropped their nuts, they can be cut and tucked into autumn and winter arrangements.

## HARVEST

Branches may be cut for flowers as soon as the catkins have become visibly elongated. Foliage and husk stems may be harvested beginning in mid- to late summer.

## POSTHARVEST

Use the flowers immediately, and expect a vase life of seven to ten days depending on harvest stage.

# *Diospyros virginiana*
## Persimmon

Persimmon trees are found in all but the coldest climates of the Southeast. In my ever-enthusiastic hunt for easily accessed cutting sources of just about anything, I've learned to recognize the presence of the fruit-laden female specimens along highways by the metallic purple sheen of their foliage. This may be either an optical result of the slight bending of fruit-heavy branches or simply their natural progression into winter dormancy. Ripe persimmon fruit has a mild, sweet flavor with a thick, jam-like texture. If it isn't ripe, the astringency will turn your mouth inside out. Wait to bite into these beauties until they smell sweet and are very soft.

### USES

Fruited persimmon branches can be used in the green stage for summer arrangements and, once they color up, in beautiful autumn arrangements. Pair with oakleaf or paniculate species such as hydrangeas, amaranth, and bittersweet. They could make an interesting subject for wreath work, but further testing is needed.

### HARVEST

Branches may be cut beginning in the green stage and continuing through their coloring up. Avoid cutting once the fruit becomes soft—they will drop and make a mess resembling dried jam wherever they land.

### POSTHARVEST

Place split stems into warm water and use immediately or store in a cooler for up to a week. Vase life varies depending on harvest stage, but can be up to one week if they are in color.

# *Fagus grandifolia*

## American Beech

Mature American beech trees cling to the earth with smooth gray roots, and their trunks and branches have a muscular look to them that is unique among our native trees. When you break a twig and chew on it, a slightly familiar flavor comes forth, and if you carve your name in its smooth trunk, it will endure for the life of the tree. The single, serrate, deep green foliage of summer gives way to coppery buff-colored leaves that hold on through the winter like fluttering angel wings. A flowering perennial species—*Epifagus virginiana*, aka beech drops—depends on the roots of the beech for survival, and if they aren't present, may signal a forest's decline in health, a virtual canary in a cage.

## USES

Winter beech leaves bring a unique color and lightness to extreme pastel arrangements, both fresh and dried, and the light gray branches they are held on never compete with even the palest of monochromatic compositions.

## HARVEST

Beech branches from smaller trees are reachable and can be harvested either as they begin to change color, to be preserved with glycerin for the most flexible enduring foliage, or can be cut into the depths of winter if the leaves are holding on.

## POSTHARVEST

To glycerinate, mix two parts warm water with one part glycerin and add the split stems. This process may take up to a month. For regular winter foliage, cut stems and store upright in a dry container. After about a week, the individual leaves can be shaped by lightly running your fingers up and down the surface, molding them as you go.

# *Hamamelis virginiana*

## Witch-hazel

Witch-hazel is a small tree with an attractive open crown shape and broadly elliptical leaves that is found in moist woodlands. It goes somewhat unnoticed beneath the towering hardwoods until late autumn when clusters of yellow flowers with strap-like petals appear along the length of the outer branches. Depending on the weather, flowering may begin while the yellow/orange autumnal foliage display is beginning to wane and continues through December, lighting up the forest when the sun is at its lowest point on the horizon.

### USES

While the foliage is still intact, witch-hazel can be added to any late autumn arrangement with other cuts of the season, such as rose hips, bittersweet, and pine. In winter, several flowering branches of witch-hazel make an elegant display on their own in a large vase.

### HARVEST

Harvest after a few of the yellow flowers become visible but while there are still plenty of buds on the branch. Branches up to three feet may be cut.

### POSTHARVEST

Place split stems into warm water. Vase life is a week. Storage is not recommended.

# Hydrangea quercifolia

## Oakleaf Hydrangea

Oakleaf hydrangea is an attractive shrub that is most frequently found in the wild along rocky riverbanks, moist woods, and streams from the Georgia/Alabama border west to Louisiana, but it is also native to the Carolinas, Tennessee, and Florida. The lobed foliage is a flat olive green that turns an interesting purple red in the fall, and the elongated, dome-shaped racemes are packed with 1-inch starry, sterile florets that slowly age from white to pink as they mature and then dry to brown. The shedding bark is cinnamon colored and stands out in winter months with the dried flower heads topping it. Its multiseasonal interest has made it a popular landscape plant, and some beautiful cultivars are available. My favorites are 'Snowflake' and 'Alice.' 'Snowflake,' a double-flowered variety, loves to be planted above a shady low wall so that its heavy blooms can gently cascade down. It originated in the Birmingham area and can be seen planted in masses there. 'Alice,' a very large-growing variety, was selected by my UGA professor, Dr. Michael Dirr, and named after

his wife. If my memory serves me correctly, I was actually on one of the plant walks through campus when Dr. Dirr noticed it growing, pointed it out, and cut a stem to remember. Vince Dooly, the legendary UGA athletic director and passionate gardener, was trailing quietly behind our group.

## USES
Oakleaf hydrangea can be used fresh or dried in large designs, including arbors. It looks beautiful with the foliage left intact and pairs well with cool minty greens, peaches, other whites, and rich plum shades.

## HARVEST
Stems may be cut once all of the petals have filled out and hardened on the entire flowering head and continuing until they are too ratty to use. Less mature stems have a better chance of staying hydrated if cut in the early morning. This hydrangea blooms on the previous season's growth, so don't cut this shrub back too hard if you want flowers the next year.

## POSTHARVEST
Split stems and condition in warm water. If there is a problem with drooping, strip the leaves and cut them again under warm water. Allow twenty-four hours for them to perk up in a cool spot. Mature flowers get the same treatment but can then be allowed to slowly dry, standing upright in water until they drink it all, or hung upside down out of sunlight.

# *Ilex* Species
## Hollies

For many of us, the word "holly" conjures either an image of pointy evergreen foliage and red berries ubiquitous to the Christmas holiday season, or a hedge—either formally pruned to be a solid fortress of small, dark green foliage or shaped individually into varying gumdrop silhouettes. The holiday variety was easy for me to draw with colored markers when I was little: three red dots surrounded by three leaves that I gave shape to by making green waves that met at the tip with a sharp point. Done. Christmas letters personalized to perfection by an eight-year-old.

# *Ilex vomitoria*

## Yaupon Holly

Although those popular images hold true, there is more to hollies than that. The yaupon holly (*Ilex vomitoria*), for instance, is the only known native North American plant that contains caffeine, and the transparent red drupes are an important food source for a range of birds.

# *Ilex glabra*

## Gallberry, Inkberry

The evergreen gallberry (*Ilex glabra*), with its inky black drupes, grows and spreads by suckers in the sandy coastal plain. Its white flowers produce loads of nectar in the spring that bees love, and the honey they produce from it is highly prized.

# Ilex decidua

## Winterberry, Possomhaw

The bright red drupes of female winterberry hollies (*Ilex decidua*) are very noticeable because, unlike many other species, this holly loses its foliage in the winter. These small trees, festooned with their brilliant fruits, brighten the dull gray landscape as far as west Texas and can be seen from nearly a mile away into the first weeks of March. This species is a great plant for the winter garden; just make sure a male cultivar selection is close by to ensure a good berry set. I must mention that the popular choice is one called 'Southern Gentleman.' I am certain whoever named it did so with a wink.

# Ilex opaca

## American Holly

The American holly (*Ilex opaca*) is a handsome evergreen tree with a conical pyramid shape in its youth. Large colonies of them can be found in the forest understory throughout the region, and it is a quintessential holly for use in holiday decor.

**USES**
The shiny green foliage of all evergreen hollies can be used as greenery any time of year. I seek out American holly trees that have turned a brighter lime green from extra sun

and cut their curving branches to bring light to both wreaths and later winter compositions. For a holiday look different from the traditional red and green, black gallberries can add the unexpected to white and green. Winterberries work well in everything except wreaths—they end up shedding their berries far more easily than durable American holly. Stuff an armload of them into a big, clear vase for a festive pop of red that will brighten a white room until Valentine's Day.

## HARVEST

Cut for foliage any time—just make sure you aren't getting the tender growth in spring. Berried branches can be harvested as soon as they are green and set, continuing until late winter. If you can, wait until the deciduous winterberry foliage has dropped before you gather it.

## POSTHARVEST

American holly and gallberry don't like extreme cold, so store in a bucket with a little water protected from direct sun and wind until you use it. If you must cut winterberry when the foliage is still on it, it can be placed in a humid cooler (or other dark, wet, cool space) for around a week to get the leaves to drop on their own; otherwise, trim them off carefully with pointy clippers.

# *Illicium floridanum*

## Florida Anise

Florida anise is an attractively rounded, 6- to 10-foot evergreen shrub found in the consistently moist soils of the Gulf Coastal Plain—from the western Florida panhandle (where it is protected), north into Georgia and Alabama, and west to the eastern toe of Louisiana. The nodding, round burgundy flowers with strappy petals are malodorous and appear in spring. The small, ornamental seedpods are shaped like stars and age from green to a woody brown. When crushed, the long oval foliage emits a pleasantly spicy aroma, giving the species its common name.

Although the native range is somewhat limited, Florida anise is hardy to zone 7 and, once established, makes a handsome landscape plant for shady areas. It can be a good substitute for gardeners that crave the mounded green presence of mountain rhododendron but live in areas where it is too hot for them to thrive. In college, I obtained a small plant of the selection 'Halley's Comet' that my professor, Dr. Michael Dirr, had rooted and brought to class. I planted it in my parents' garden in Moultrie, Georgia, moved it once, and have watched it grow for over twenty years into a 9-by-12-foot specimen that looks beautiful twelve months out of the year. *Illicium parviflorum* (yellow anisetree) is a species cousin that is slightly smaller in stature with more vertically pointing foliage. The nativar 'Florida Sunshine' has excellent chartreuse foliage that I can only dream of growing in my zone 6 garden.

## USES
The smooth, slightly floppy foliage is a great evergreen base for arrangements and looks handsome out of water for days, lending itself to large installations. The starry fruits can be used in long-lasting dried arrangements and wreaths.

## HARVEST
Foliage stems can be cut anytime if the new growth has hardened off. The anise stars can be cut when green for fresh use and are best gathered for dried use in autumn after they have aged to brown. Due to the unpleasant smell, the flowers are not recommended for floral design.

## POSTHARVEST
Place split foliage stems into warm water and use within a week for a vase life up to fourteen days. Cold storage is not necessary. Remove foliage from stems with the aged stars, cure upright in an open, dry container, and store flat for up to six months.

# *Itea virginica*
## Virginia Sweetspire

*Itea* is a lovely deciduous shrub that is frequently found along the edges of ponds and slow-moving rivers and creeks. Although a wetland plant by nature, it has proved itself to be forgiving of less-than-ideal conditions and has found its way into popular cultivation due to its abundance of hanging, white, 3- to 5-inch bottlebrush-shaped flowers, arching habit, and gorgeous yellow to garnet fall color. There are several popular selections available commercially, and my favorite for cutting is 'Saturn.' *Itea* spreads slowly by suckers and is best planted in masses for the awesome seasonal effects.

## USES

Branches of blooms are an excellent way to bring a waterfall of movement in any mixed composition. The colorful autumn foliage has the same sense of movement—situate it low in a tall vase to hang down, or let it explode from the side or top.

## HARVEST

Harvest flowering branches from the time buds are completely white until the open flowers begin to brown and fade.

## POSTHARVEST

Split stems and store in water. Depending on harvest stage, vase life is five to ten days.

# *Juniperus virginiana*

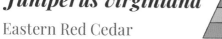      

## Eastern Red Cedar

Large populations of this evergreen tree dot the landscape throughout the Southeast except for the very high mountains. This plant shows its genetic diversity from one plant to the next even in a single population: You can find silvery-foliaged, loosely pyramidal trees growing right next to limey green, conical specimens, and even trees that sport stripes of gold on their foliage. Populations closest to the coast typically exhibit brighter green foliage on dense, squatty plants. The small berries vary in appearance almost as much as the foliage, from bright navy blue to waxy silver sky blue. The one drawback to relying on this plant from one year to the next is the fact that by population, they are only covered in berries once every three years. On off years, you might find one in a thousand that has berries, although I have noticed that the commercial selection 'Brodie' has berries more often. (You can thank that observation to a large planting of them around the back of a local Walmart that

I have hit year after year in order to maintain photographic consistency of my wreaths. I am doing them a favor, really; if it weren't for my consistent and thoughtful trimming, the 18-wheelers might not be able to back in and out properly.)

## USES

This wonderfully scented cedar is indispensable in winter floral designs, providing long-lasting foliage for wreaths, garlands, and arrangements. *Juniperus virginiana* is a perfect addition to winter wedding bouquets.

## HARVEST

Seek out individual trees that have the qualities you are after, such as heavy berries, a particular coloration of the needles, or even the density of the foliage—from feathery and light to more concentrated and substantial. Branches can be cut 6 to 36 inches long.

## POSTHARVEST

Cedar harvested for wreath work in late fall and winter should be stored outside on the ground on the north-facing side of a building or other deeply shaded area and used within two weeks. Covering the branches with the white shade cloth used on Christmas tree farms and occasional misting may extend its life. Use immediately if daytime temps are regularly above 75°F. Branches trimmed to 12 inches can be split and put in water with a vase life ranging from a week to a month, depending on where it is placed. Life expectancy indoors above an actively used fireplace, woodstove, or near a heater is about a week before it becomes a possible fire hazard. Greens used outside can last anywhere from three weeks to three months depending on the climate.

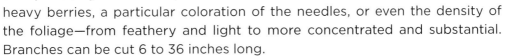

# *Kalmia latifolia*
## Mountain Laurel

Despite its common name, mountain laurel can be found growing naturally all the way down to Gulf Coast counties, from Florida (where they are listed as threatened) to Mississippi. In the mountains, it prefers the drier and sunnier south- and west-facing slopes. Farther south, it is more likely to be found growing along with magnolia, ilex, and illicium on cool shaded banks,

slopes, and ridges above moving water. My guess is these southern populations found their way down from the mountains over eons by the distribution of seeds via south-flowing waterways and slowly adapted to the different climate through generations. To me, this species is a primary indicator that the entire Southeast is tied together botanically regardless of the very different geography, geology, and climate from one regional plant community to the next. If you want mountain laurel growing in your garden, seek out sources that have propagated plants from local populations—especially down south.

## USES

Mountain laurel makes a fine addition to late spring/early summer arrangements and can be cut slightly early for forcing. They hold extremely well in large-scale installations and are stunning mixed with other light pinks and white flowers as well as buttery yellow.

## HARVEST

Mountain laurel is best harvested before you see it lighting up the landscape, because by then some of the individual flowers are ready to drop. Unless they are being forced, cut stems when the buds resemble the funky dried icing flowers one buys at the grocery store for box-made cupcakes when a best friend's birthday was forgotten. The flowers are very sticky and need to be placed upright in a container right after you have a handful, rather than piled up in the back of your car. I am completely guilty of the second and always pay for it in blossom loss—learn from my mistakes!

**POSTHARVEST**

Use immediately and expect a vase life of a week when you cut as suggested. Otherwise, store in a cooler for up to three weeks for a four-day vase life.

# *Liriodendron tulipifera*

## Tulip Poplar

Tulip poplars are a fast-growing pioneer tree that can dominate a young forest in some locales. The green and cantaloupe orange, cup-shaped flowers are what give this tree its common name, but it is actually in the magnolia family—not a true poplar. Since they are tall trees, the bloom isn't necessarily in your face and may go unnoticed until hundreds of shriveled petals start to cover the earth below their high canopy. I may not ever have considered this as a viable cut if it weren't for a small branch that came down and landed in a ditch directly across from a turn I often take when foraging. It was loaded with beautiful teardrop buds, and I felt they shouldn't go to waste. That was a good decision and a perfect lesson of my philosophy that everything is fair game.

**USES**

In the late weeks of spring, tulip poplar branches lend structure, soft color, and an air of surprise to medium to large garden-style arrangements, and also stand alone or with one or two other species for Ikebana compositions. I pair it with snowball viburnum, flame azaleas, and black cherry blossoms. Try mixing it with pale peach poppies or ranunculus.

**HARVEST**

Seek out trees that have recently fallen or those with branches that are closer to the ground, or use pole pruners and a ladder. Cut thinner branches with buds situated in a manner you prefer. Unless you are using them for a massive installation, 1- to 2-foot stems work best, as they can be heavy without cage support.

**POSTHARVEST**

Put cut and split stems into cold water for storage or warm for immediate use. Branches with buds can be held in a cooler for up to two weeks. Vase life is five to seven days.

# *Magnolia* Species

## *Magnolia fraseri*
### Cucumber Tree

*Magnolia fraseri*, or cucumber tree, the deciduous magnolia of the mountains, is a medium-sized tree with a handsome oval form. Its large white blooms appear before the large leaves emerge—not long after the serviceberries bloom in spring—and it can be truly appreciated when viewed from an opposing hillside. I'm lucky enough to have that viewpoint from my kitchen window, and wait for

its appearance annually. If you are able to reach a few blooms with clippers, they are worth the effort.

# *Magnolia grandiflora*
## Southern Magnolia

With their dark, shiny evergreen foliage and big, lemon-scented ivory flowers, southern magnolias—*Magnolia grandiflora*—need little introduction. These iconic trees of the Deep South belong to the most primitive family of flowering plants—Magnoliaceae—which were around long before there were bees flying. This species populates low areas and deep woods of the coastal plain by nature. Populations exhibit variants in both the size and color of the foliage: from waxy to deep green on top and from gray to velvety tobacco brown on the underside. Southern magnolias have been cultivated in gardens for generations, providing shade and beauty through the seasons, and thus naturalized itself in the Piedmont from those plantings.

I will always remember my mother telling me she wanted magnolia blossoms when she got married in the late 1960s and was told she couldn't have them. I still don't understand why she was denied that *very* basic request; it's not like they had to be flown in from some exotic locale. Goodness, they were probably blooming their heads off that June in Dawson, Georgia. If I had been in charge of the flowers for that beautiful lady, she would have had magnolia blossoms. Dream flowers or not, everything ended well—my parents are still in love over fifty years later.

# *Magnolia virginiana*
## Sweetbay Magnolia

*Magnolia virginiana*, or sweetbay magnolia, is an evergreen species with foliage that is smaller and narrower than the other two species just described. When the wind blows, their olive-toned leaves reveal a silver underside. Crush them in your hand, take a sniff, and you'll know why they have "bay" in their common name—it's reminiscent of bay leaves. They grow naturally in the wetter areas of lower altitudes, and cultivated selections are excellent in the landscape—I particularly like the multibranched specimens. The flowers are like a mini version of *Magnolia grandiflora* with a characteristic lemon scent.

## USES

If cut at the right time, magnolias provide the blossoms that every mother dreams of, although they are short lived and easily bruised. Buds that are just about to open or have unfurled their petals that morning can be floated in a shallow vessel of water (I prefer silver for reflective purposes), or a short stem can be secured in a pin frog attached to a vase that is small but weighty enough not to tip over from the heavy bloom. This applies to all native magnolia blossoms, although the sweetbay blossoms may be small enough to use multiflowered stems.

Southern magnolia foliage is excellent in wreaths and as the lower component of large arrangements, but you already knew that! I like using sweetbay branches for similar purposes but with a lighter effect.

## HARVEST

To avoid bruising the large, thick petals, cut magnolia blossoms in bud when they are at full oval teardrop stage—not too tight. Hardened foliage can be snapped off by hand. I usually go for the whorled clusters deep in the understory unless a tree farm tells me to go for it because the tree will be bulldozed. If that is the case, I take pole pruners and show no mercy. Warning: If you butcher most of a southern magnolia's foliage for the sake of Christmas decor, you are likely to have no magnolia the next year (or ever again), so trim with prudence unless the plant is slated for destruction.

## POSTHARVEST

Magnolia blossoms are best used immediately. If it is necessary, store stems with the flower still in the bud stage in a 38°F cooler for no more than four days. Vase life is two to three days. Magnolia foliage can be temporarily held for up to two weeks on the ground out of sunlight (the north side of a building is a great spot!). If it is very dry, give them a biweekly shower of water. If temperatures are below 28°F, cover the foliage lightly with a tarp or lightly pack the stems into large black trash bags and continue to store in the shade until needed. Southern magnolia leaves can stick around for years, but after three or four weeks, the glossy green will begin to fade.

## Malus angustifolia
### Southern Crabapple

Native crabapples are small trees with sweet-smelling, clear pink flowers in the spring that are followed by small red-green fruits. Although the fruits are too sour to eat fresh, they make great jam or jelly. During the bloom, they set themselves apart from the rest of the native fruiting trees, which primarily have white blooms, and escaped peach trees, which have pink flowers that are much bigger. They are scattered throughout the region in woodland borders, thickets, and old fence lines.

### USES

Spring-harvested branches have an interesting structure. I like the peachy glow they have right after the petals have dropped and mix them with Carolina jessamine and *Cornus florida*. Fruited branches can be used in any fall designs and are great tucked into wreaths for the holidays.

### HARVEST

Cut flowers any time—from barely visible bud stage for forcing, until after the petals have dropped. Cut fruited branches in autumn when foliage begins to turn.

### POSTHARVEST

For forcing branches, place cut and split stems into warm water and bring inside where the temps are warmer (65°F) and the air isn't too dry for a few days until you see the buds swelling; they may then be arranged. Blooming branches should be used immediately. Vase life depends on the stage of harvest. Fruited branches will keep best if used in outdoor decor or very temporary arrangements indoors.

# *Myrica cerifera*
## Waxmyrtle

Waxmyrtle is a large, broadleaf evergreen shrub or small tree that is most often found in the wild growing along ponds, ditches, and bogs but has been used as an ornamental throughout the lower altitudes of the region. My first experience with waxmyrtle was as a child fishing in our pond. My dad taught me how to pick the leaves and rub them vigorously between my hands—releasing the bay-scented oils and getting rid of (or at least camouflaging) the fishy smell incurred from removing dinner from the hook.

### USES

The long-lasting, olive-green foliage can be used as a substitute for true olive. My favorite part is the branches covered all the way around with tiny silver berries. They are situated far enough below the whorled leaves to make it easy to trim the foliage away, and what remains lends a frosty look to bouquets, arrangements, wreaths, swags, and arbors.

## HARVEST

Branches can be cut for foliage any time of year. If harvesting for seeded branches, cut from early fall through deep winter when the silver berries have matured.

## POSTHARVEST

For fresh use, cut and split stems and place in warm water. Vase life is up to two weeks if kept hydrated. For dried use, snip away leaves at the top of each branch and any others that may impede the berry display, and store upright in a dry place. Dried branches with berries last one year or more.

# *Oxydendrum arboreum*

Sourwood

Sourwood is a tough little tree whose warm, blushing foliage and large sprays of white flowers in summer are easily spotted along roadsides and clearings. They survive baking clay soil and multiple cuttings by the DOT, making them an ideal specimen for some of the toughest growing conditions. The white flowers provide ample pollen for bees, and sourwood honey is some of the finest out there.

## USES

Sourwood foliage is absolutely one of my favorite native cuts. It works well in vases and bouquets and holds in floral foam for large-scale installations like arbors. The leaves display ideal shades of rosy terracotta, which not only

provides a backdrop for brilliant red, violet, and rust flowers but also comple- ments soft pastels and deeper-toned burgundies. Pair with the seed heads of various grasses, aster, phlox, aging hydrangeas, verbena, zinnias, yarrow, and dahlias. The flowers and subsequent seed heads, though usually out of reach, can bring movement to any arrangement.

## HARVEST

Stems can be cut for foliage beginning in June. The most effective cuts are 14 to 24 inches long and come from the top of the plant where the color is best. Flowers can be harvested any time after they are visible.

## POSTHARVEST

Stems should be split and diagonally cut, then placed into warm water. Sour- wood foliage lasts longer and resists drooping when stems are given an over- night period to fully hydrate before arranging. Both foliage and flowers have a vase life of fourteen days.

# *Philadelphus inodorus*
## Mock Orange

Across the Southeast, in very late spring, the occasionally large colonies of mock orange are easily seen cascading down banks and lighting up roadsides with their pure white flowers. In the mountains, the wild display begins just before the invasive multiflora roses bloom and disappears almost as magically as it appeared. There are also cultivars of mock orange to be found around old home sites, whose botanical lineage is somewhat vague, but I include them in this description because locating them may be easier. These tend to have larger flowers and a pleasingly sweet scent reminiscent of orange blossoms. This large shrub sets flower clusters at the end points of the previous year's growth. Cutting long branches of mock orange encourages fresh vegetative growth and therefore more flowers the next season.

## USES

Due to the flowering season and color, mock orange is widely used in wed- ding work but certainly shouldn't be limited to that. Long, flowering branches stuffed into a big vase can stand alone as a statement, and short stems are perfect tucked into lower arrangements with seasonal flowers such as ranun- culus, amsonia, baptisia, and snapdragons. Little pieces that are still in bud are perfect for boutonnieres, wrist corsages, and flowery hair combs just in time for prom season.

## HARVEST

Harvest when branches have visible white buds and some of the flowers on the plant are beginning to open.

## POSTHARVEST

If long branches are to be used, place cut and split stems into warm water. Smaller stems, 1 inch and under, do not need this treatment. Use immediately or store at 38°F for up to three weeks. If storing, remove two-thirds of the foliage to increase longevity and slow dehydration.

# *Physocarpus opulifolius*
## Ninebark

Ninebark is a deciduous shrub that can be found most often growing along the banks of rivers in the cooler realms of the mountains and upper Piedmont region. The 1- to 2-inch trident foliage has a corrugated appearance, and the peeling bark of the stems further distinguishes it from other waterside species. It is more typical of ecosystems in Missouri and more northeastern states, but when found growing in the Southeast, it is in thick bankside colonies.

## USES

The cascading branches of ninebark provide movement and texture through three seasons. Spring yields white flower clusters along entire branches, summer brings rosy-colored seed clusters and lovely dark lime-green serrated foliage, and the entire display culminates in autumn when the green gives way to a golden yellow. Excellent both as a structural base in smaller arrangements and for shooting and arching out of very large ones, this is a native that crosses the board. It performs well for two to three days in floral foam as long as it receives a soaking once or twice a day.

## HARVEST
Cut stems can be harvested 14 to 36 inches long once the foliage has emerged in the spring and may continue until foliage begins to drop in autumn.

## POSTHARVEST
Ninebark performs best when stems are recut and split then hydrated in warm water. Keep in mind that this is a plant that thrives near rivers, and, consequently, loves to drink water. Vase life is about seven days.

# *Prunus serotina*

## Black Cherry

Black cherries are trees that are most easily spotted along roadsides and other woodland edges. Their flowers appear much later than those of other fruiting trees, after the foliage has fully emerged.

## USES
Branches of black cherry flowers are beautiful in late spring arrangements with other natives. They can be part of a green-and-white ensemble or mixed in with soft shades of yellow and orange like tulip poplar flowers or flame azaleas. Although they can be cut down for low centerpieces, they truly shine on the outermost edges of large arrangements.

## HARVEST

Cut branches 1 to 3 feet before the flowers open, when the sprays are visible with light, hanging clusters of tiny white balls.

## POSTHARVEST

Split stems and hydrate in warm water. Use immediately or store in a cooler for up to ten days.

# *Rhododendron* Species

## Rhododendron and Azaleas

The over nine hundred species that make up the *Rhododendron* genus are commonly known as either rhododendron or azaleas, and a nearly endless number of cultivars exist because they are easily hybridized. Along with China and Japan, the eastern United States is fortunate to be home to some of the world's most colorful and useful species, and I am covering only a handful of this beautiful group of native plants.

# *Rhododendron arborescens*

## Sweet Azalea

When I first encountered a sweet azalea growing wild along the banks of the Watauga River, I smelled it long before I saw it. The pure white flowers are accented with red stamens on this large shrub, and the sweet perfume scent emanating from them in June is nothing short of heavenly.

# *Rhododendron calendulaceum*

## Flame Azalea

Deciduous flame azaleas can be found growing wild throughout the Appalachian region, and their genetic diversity becomes apparent when they explode into bloom in late spring. Plants cover themselves with blooms varying in burning shades of yellow to orange to almost red. The flower sizes can also differ noticeably from one plant to the next when observed scattered on rocky hillsides below open forest canopies. Plants grown from wild collected seed or selected cultivars make wonderful additions to any garden with cooler summers. *Rhododendron austrinum*, the Florida flame azalea, has similar coloration and grows wild on the Gulf Coastal Plain. If you want to introduce these brilliant plants to your garden, cultivars of this more heat-tolerant species are a better option.

# Rhododendron canescens
## Piedmont or Florida Pinxter Azalea

*Rhododendron canescens* are the most abundant species of the Southeast. Their stoloniferous habit allows them to form colonies in open woods, old fields, and streamsides. I have encountered large groups of them growing only 2 or 3 feet high but loaded with long, flowering stems. Their sweetly scented pink flowers are visible in March and April.

# Rhododendron maximum
## Rosebay

Finally, *Rhododendron maximum*, the stately shrub with big, deeply evergreen, pointy oval leaves and light pink to white flowers in July, characterizes the shady mountain hillsides of southern Appalachia. They form thickets so dense that they were dubbed "hells" by early settlers due to their impassability.

### USES
The flowers of this genus are striking enough to be the focal point of arrangements and mix well with whatever other natives are blooming at the time.

Rosebay foliage makes a great-looking wreath and is a good substitute for southern magnolia in the mountains.

## HARVEST

Flower stems are best harvested from the time the buds are colored and full through the stage at which most of the flowers are fully opened. Before you cut, give the branch a shake; if all of the petals drop, it's too late. On

larger plants, I like to cut 1- to 3-foot branches that have a shapely curve. With smaller-growing types, I select erect stems with upward-facing inflorescences. Cut stems for foliage at any time—go for the most compact-looking leaves that are on the upper part of the plant or facing more light.

## POSTHARVEST

Split flowering stems and condition them in warm water. I have experimented with holding sweet azaleas in a walk-in cooler at 38–40°F and they have kept for over a month, although I would not recommend it. If you really need to hold them, store budded stems that are about to burst open for up to a week. Vase life can range from three to seven days, depending on stage of harvest. Foliage used in a wreath during winter will stay green for three weeks if hung out of direct sunlight.

# *Rhus glabra*
Smooth Sumac

Smooth sumac is a small tree that forms short-lived, often suckering colonies along roadsides and neglected clearings. This is a plant that comes and goes within the span of ten years in one area or sporadically pops up continuously in close proximity to previous generations. The seed heads punctuate the sky with giant, elongated drops of deep crimson set atop the spare architecture of their brittle branches. An autumn spectrum of orange to brilliant red notifies one of their presence in advance of harvest time. The clusters are extremely long lasting—often persisting on the tree into the next season's harvest—unless they are knocked over by strong winds, animals, or the DOT. The seeds of smooth sumac are also edible and were flavoring dishes and drinks with a vitamin C–packed tang long before European settlers found their way here.

## USES

The velvet seed heads of smooth sumac are excellent, long-lasting additions to wreaths, swags, and other holiday decorations. They balance the visual heft of southern magnolia foliage and look rich against a backdrop of golden evergreens from autumn through the new year.

## HARVEST

*Rhus glabra* heads are most easily harvested fresh in fall once all of the leaves have changed from green. At this stage, the compound pinnate foliage is easily removed almost as you harvest. Use pole pruners to cut them about 9 inches below the base of the head, and take care not to break branches. Always leave plenty of seed heads for birds to find and help establish new colonies.

## POSTHARVEST

Remove any remaining foliage. Store out of water in a dry place either laid flat or upright.

# *Rosa palustris*

Swamp Rose

I know that every rose has its thorn, but swamp roses have *very* big thorns. There is no doubt in my mind that those thorns are there to defend the huge, shiny red "hips" (berries) that adorn the plants. The thorns do their job well, and the fruits often persist well into February before a bird or mammal gets hungry enough to brave the pain. No pain, no gain in the world of foraging—these rounded beauties are the most spectacular and long-lasting red berries out there. Colonies of swamp roses are found in sunny low spots and along streams. A similar species, *Rosa Carolina*, or field rose, can be found on slightly higher ground.

## USES

Perfect for any type of winter decor, wrap swamp rose into wreaths with evergreen foliage and other berries and cones, tuck into vase arrangements, or add to outdoor planters that have been dressed for the season.

## HARVEST

Use leather gloves and harvest 12-inch stems when the hips are bright red. Hips that are harvested when green to orange or when the foliage is still intact will shrivel quickly out of water, but can be used in fall arrangements if in water.

## POSTHARVEST

To ease tangling and breakage, store mature stems of hip clusters either upright in a wide bucket or separately laid out on a flat surface. Caution: If rose hips are lying around within easy reach of small mammals, they are an easy target due to their high nutrient content and fetching color. The little thieves can make a big shiny pile of red disappear overnight only to be found months later stowed away where you least expect it.

# *Rubus* Species

Members of the genus *Rubus* number in the hundreds, so many that the scientific study of these brambles has its own name—"batology"—derived from the Greek word *báton*, which means "blackberry." I would hardly have room to cover the dozens of species that are found in the Southeast (and I'm no batologist), but I do have several favorites for floral design that are uniquely beautiful.

# *Rubus argutus*

## Blackberry

This broad group of species is the more commonly found bramble in the coastal plain and Piedmont areas. Blackberries possess the characteristic thorny, arching canes that are covered in white blooms in the spring before transitioning from green to red to shining black fruit. It is worth braving those thorns, whether you are picking for cobblers and jam or cutting the loaded stems for a lush arrangement. If the thought of those thorns makes you less inclined, think of their cousin, the rose, and what you do to get your hands on those blooms, then remember these wild lovelies aren't covered in chemicals to keep them happy.

## *Rubus flagellaris*

### Dewberry

Dewberries are another catchall term for a group of species that produce tasty blackberries similar to blackberries but, for the sake of this book, are differentiated by their thin, trailing stems that hug the ground. They are found growing in a variety of terrains and locales: I've picked them or cut the stems on the Gulf Coast in April and done the same thing in early June in the Appalachian Mountains.

## *Rubus occidentalis*

### Black Raspberry

Black raspberries, being a more predominantly northern species, grow wild in the mountains, the upper Piedmont of North Carolina, and almost all of

Virginia. This attractive species cascades loosely down banksides and is easily recognized in the winter by its waxy lavender to almost pink canes that have fewer thorns than the blackberries. In early summer, attractive foliage with silver undersides complements the then powdery blue stems and red to black berries.

# *Rubus odoratus*

## Thimbleberry

Thimbleberry is probably one of the most striking members of the *Rubus* genus in our region. The large green leaves along the 5-foot-tall cinnamon-colored stems are the perfect backdrop for its large, bright pink flowers. Although the fruit isn't plentiful, it is beyond delicious and, better yet, not a single thorn to be found. This beauty is commonly found growing in colonies on rocky, partially shaded banks and forest glens in the mountains alongside *Hydrangea arborescens*. It is definitely worth considering as an addition to any mountain garden, provided it is given room to spread. Native bees absolutely love feeding on its nectar, and I have wasted far too much time filming them doing just that on the buckets of cuts I've brought home.

### USES

The *Rubus* species can be used in various ways in accordance with their habits and the season at hand. The colorful canes of black raspberry can be added to winter wreaths and container designs. Dewberries can trail out and down vases both large and small—particularly when they are blooming or have set fruit. Blackberries, with their masses of white flowers and strong canes, can erupt from spring ensembles or add luscious weight to summer mixes when they are laden with juicy fruit. The large thimbleberry foliage is a great base to large arrangements, and its loose clusters of flowers and fruit can even be tucked into bouquets as small, colorful additions to larger, round flowers.

## HARVEST

Aside from the thimbleberry, use gloves to cut the stems of this genus. Bare canes can be harvested whenever they are dormant. Canes and trailers that are harvested for flowers are best done when about a third of the flowers are open. Fruited stems are best gathered from the time the berries are visible and green until they are black and hard. Don't wait until they are too ripe or you will have a mess!

## POSTHARVEST

Place cut actively growing stems into warm water. Store in water in a cooler at about 42°F for up to a week if necessary. Vase life is about seven days. Bare canes can be stored on the ground outside until ready to use. They will stay bright for at least a month without water.

# *Sambucus canadensis*
## Elderberry

American elders begin to highlight roadsides and well-drained low-lying areas in early summer with big, lacy white umbels. Underneath these thicket-forming shrubs, birds like quail and grouse find a safe hideaway with their young. The berries that begin to ripen in July to August are enjoyed by dozens of animal species. If you have ever read *The Secret Life of Bees* by Sue Monk Kidd, you may recall those South Carolina beekeepers talking about elderberry honey. When the sweltering heat of late summer leaves few blooming sources of nectar, the bees feed on the juice of ripe elderberries, and the honey they produce from that is purple. I've never come across a jar of elderberry honey, but I sure do love to use those berries in arrangements from the time the green clusters begin to give way to just a hint purple until about a week before they are ripe enough to eat.

## USES

Elderberry clusters signify abundance, and they are a great textural addition spilling forth from the edge of a vase. If they aren't as ripe, they can be placed

higher. Bouquets that are more rounded in form can also benefit from their presence, and they look smashing with blush, white, blackberry, peach, and juicy coral shades.

## HARVEST
Harvest just as the green berries begin to blush purple. The heads are somewhat brittle, so I cut shorter stems with one cluster each to avoid breaking them. Although it is tempting to use the flowers, resist the urge—they droop quickly and aren't worth trying to rehydrate—and wait for the berries.

## POSTHARVEST
Place split stems into warm water and use within a day or two. Vase life is up to a week depending on berry stage.

# *Sassafras albidum*
## Sassafras

The minty lime-green flower clusters of sassafras appear in early spring right about the same time that *Cornus florida* flowers are beginning to become visible in the same way. In the mountains, it is a tree that forms colonies and puts on a spectacular display in autumn at the forest's edge. On the coastal plain, where my father once showed me how a piece of the root could be used as a tasty toothbrush, it is more of a shrub. The roots are also traditionally used to make root beer, and the young leaves are dried and ground to make filé powder—which, if you know what gumbo is, you know is essential to finish the soup properly.

## USES

The early season flowers bring a bright, almost chartreuse touch to any arrangement, either cut short or left tall for single species displays. The 5-inch, smooth, three-lobed foliage is good backdrop green in summer, and the purple, red, orange, and yellow autumn foliage can knock your socks off in autumn compositions.

## HARVEST

Both flowers and foliage can be cut as soon as they catch your eye and you have a plan for them.

## POSTHARVEST

After splitting stems in warm water, both flowers and foliage will look good in water for up to ten days.

# *Symphoricarpos orbiculatus*

Coralberry, Indian Currant

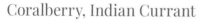    

Coralberry is a small, deciduous, 4-foot shrub that spreads by suckers. It can be found on the western side of the Blue Ridge Mountains, the North Carolina Piedmont, middle Tennessee, and all of Virginia. The shedding, cinnamon-colored branches give way to loosely arching stems with small, oppositely arranged oval leaves. The shiny fuchsia-pink berries of this shrub, which begin to shine after a few cold snaps in autumn, are like nothing else I have ever seen and rival those of beautyberry. Like beautyberry, they bloom and set fruit on new growth—meaning the more you cut, the better the yield the following

year. I find that the roadside colonies where the DOT mows them annually are the best for foraging because of this.

## USES
Coralberries can last for weeks—even months—in a vase of water by themselves, and may even put out roots in the water. The fuchsia color will fade to a deeper shade of cranberry after a couple of weeks inside, but they are positively brilliant when mixed with anything from bright lime holly foliage, cryptomeria, berried juniper branches, magnolia foliage, witch-hazel, gold false cypress, privet berries, and all the way to bittersweet branches. If it is available to you, take advantage of it for wreaths and any other early winter floral designs where some juicy pink is just the ticket!

## HARVEST
Cut 1- to 2-foot branched sprays when the berries are shining pink. The foliage may get in the way and I usually wait until it has dropped before I cut it.

## POSTHARVEST
Coralberry likes to be hydrated, and although I gather armfuls at a time for wreath work, I always store them in a bucket of water.

# *Vaccinium* Species

Various species of blueberries can be found growing in acidic soils throughout the Southeast—some growing low to the ground, others reaching 15 feet, and all making their presence known in autumn when the rounded foliage turns red. The springtime flowers are white hanging bells that give way to clusters of rounded, waxy fruits ripening from green to pink to blue.

*Vaccinium myrsinites*

*Vaccinium corymbosum*

## *Vaccinium corymbosum*

Blueberry

## *Vaccinium myrsinites*

Shiny Blueberry

### USES

Devoid of foliage, the shapely, thin green stems bring a fairy-like touch with their hanging flowers to spring compositions and can be mixed with the rosy seed clusters of maple, Carolina jessamine, and dogwood. Berried stems are great additions for both color and texture to monochromatic compositions in shades of ivory, blush, peach, or yellow.

## HARVEST
Cut flowering stems when they are visible. For fruited stems, it is best to harvest before they are fully ripe in order to avoid berries dropping all over the place. For hydration purposes, they are best cut from stalks that aren't too old and woody looking.

## POSTHARVEST
The light flowering stems have a vase life of four to seven days. The berried stems need to be carefully stripped of foliage, split, and placed in warm water for a vase life of seven days.

# Design

Now that you've become familiar with the abundant supply of gorgeous native cuts available and the tricks of harvesting them, it's time to play! The following series of designs showcases native plants through the seasons, from the mountains to the coast and back again. Some are exclusively native compositions, while others may include other foraged non-natives, nativars, and cut flowers grown on my farm. The intention of these series is to demonstrate how useful native plants can have a place in floral design and to spark your creative juices. I am not a formally trained floral designer, but I have been working with these materials for decades and have learned a few tricks along the way. Whether you are just dipping your toes into the world of locally gathered or grown flowers or a seasoned florist, I am sure you will find inspiration and insightful knowledge that you can apply to your native designs.

# SPRING TUTORIALS

THE EMERGENCE OF SPRING HAS MANY FACES as it marches from the barely freezing most southerly areas in February, through the Piedmont by April, and all the way up to the mountain peaks by late May. I always think of spring being like a teenage party at your parents' house when they aren't home: At first, a few close friends show up and things are quietly low key. After that, a few more folks knock on the door and the anticipation builds. Before you realize what is happening, the place is packed, spilling out onto the grass, the music is blaring, and things are really happening. The party reaches its peak, the neighbors start to complain, and the cacophony slowly fades into memory. In nature, the canopy of green leaves close in and the long days of summer settle in.

I'll do just about anything for flowers and foliage this time of year, and once in hand, I make the most of them.

## Miniature Bowl Gardens

The ephemeral blossoms of early spring make themselves at home with collections of bright green and gray mosses that have been plumped by the cold rains of the season. One of my favorite things to find while I'm roaming the woods are old glass bottles, long forgotten, filled with squishy, thriving moss and the occasional flowering plant. Spontaneous wild terrariums hold a special kind of magic. Captivating tiny versions of the big picture have spurred me to assemble my own little landscapes for as long as I can remember. They are charming and can last quite a long while if you use my newest tactic of building on a base of old floral foam (which is a good way to recycle it) that I learned from my flower friend Carolyn. She's a now-retired floral designer who loves resurrection ferns, and the bowl garden she made for an event five years ago is still going on a table on her back deck. If you want to make arrangements like this and want them to stick around, make sure they are outside and shaded when not displayed inside. The moss shades the roots, and the foam oasis keeps them hydrated but not waterlogged.

## MATERIALS

Moss, reindeer moss, violets, resurrection fern, club (arborvitae) moss, moss phlox, wintergreen, heuchera, colt's foot, asarum (wild ginger), snakeroot, carex. Seriously, whatever you can find growing this time of year that is interesting and doesn't have a deep root system will do!

## ASSEMBLY

**1.** Hydrate the floral foam: Fill a bucket halfway or more with warm water and set the floral foam on the surface of the water. Allow the foam to hydrate and sink to the bottom of the bucket over the course of a couple of hours. Don't push the foam down into the water—that creates unwanted air pockets. (This soaking method applies to any time you hydrate foam—old or new.)

**2.** While the foam is soaking, take a hike. Take a set of clippers, a small trowel or hand mattock, and something to carry your goodies in. Hit the woods and carefully gather a nice selection of moss, little ferns, and whatever else catches your eye—such as tiny flowering annuals, plants with interesting foliage, grass-like sedges, and a few sprigs of running groundcover. Make sure you get their roots, and don't be greedy—these tiny landscapes don't need much. I also like to add a cut branch to two if any catch my eye and are the right proportion.

**3.** When you return from your foraging mission, lay everything you gathered out on something flat and give them a good soak with the hose or kitchen sprayer. This helps them hydrate and recover from the trauma digging may have caused.

**4.** Gather several shallow waterproof containers that look good together; I like using vintage milk glass pieces.

**5.** Cut pieces of the floral foam to fit each container—it's okay to patch pieces together to use the entire foam block.

**6.** Set the foam in snugly in each vessel.

**7.** Cover the tops of the containers with moss. Although it's fine to use several types of moss, each individual container will look better if you stick to just one kind or at least keep them in solid blocks if they vary—it's more convincing that way. Don't worry if it looks patchy—you will need openings when you begin adding plants, and you can always touch up with more moss at the end.

**8.** Once you are satisfied with the moss, begin with the most structural plants you've gathered. The roots need to be under the moss for support and somewhat pressed into the foam oasis, so they stay hydrated and have a surface on which to grow.

Continue to add more plants, creating layers and little "stories" as you go. Be mindful of both the scale and proportion for each individual container and also how they relate as a whole.

**9.** After all of the containers have been filled and the moss has been adjusted, stand back and take a look. Does it seem like something is missing? In this grouping, I felt like the green vase wasn't quite right and it was detracting from the rest of the mini gardens.

**10.** To finish the entire group, I added several stems of *Cornus mas* that I found on my foraging hike. The tiny yellow flowers had just begun to show their buds, and the rather delicate branches had an airy movement about them. In order to maintain a good scale, cut branches like this down so their height is about one and one-third the height and diameter of the container they are in. Bunch them together to maintain a realistic point of origin and gently stick them into the floral foam—one at a time but keeping the tight grouping.

**11.** After your mini gardens are complete, top them with a little bit of water and enjoy! These will last about a week inside as long as you don't let them dry out. When they begin to look leggy, take them outside and display them on a table that is in the shade. Don't forget to water them during very dry spells!

## Spring Spectrum

SPRING FLOWERS EXPRESS THE SAME EXCITEMENT that the sight of a rainbow does after a good rain has washed away the tree pollen. This design came about because I wanted to make something that looked as if a flower rainbow was rocketing out of a grassy meadow. Arranging in a graduated spectrum when there is this much color going on makes more sense to the eyes than does a jumble of color scattered willy-nilly. This long, low design is easy to assemble and can make the perfect centerpiece for a rectangular table set to celebrate the renewal of life this time of year. The trick is to gather all of your materials—keeping in mind not only colors but ideal shapes and lengths for the high and low parts. Once you have gathered everything you want to use, lay it out on the table in a rainbow (or even a monochromatic spectrum) and make any color tweaks you need to before putting it all together. ***Note:*** I changed backgrounds while I was making this because I loved seeing how the spectrum played out on each. The lesson: Rainbows look good with anything!

## MATERIALS
I used whatever I could find, and you can too!

- Green: Fresh pine needle branches for the "grass"
- Yellow: *Cornus mas*, sarracenia, Carolina jessamine, golden ragwort
- Orange to red: 'Twinny Peach' snapdragon, columbine, flame honeysuckle, red flowering dogwood, maple tree branches with colored seed clusters, silene (fire pinks, which are a true *red*—go figure)
- Pink to purple: Pinxter azalea, peach, red bud, Japanese magnolia
- Blue: Spiderwort, erigeron

## ASSEMBLY

**1.** Select a long, low, rectangular or oval vessel and insert a piece of chicken wire that has been rolled into a loose tube and cut the same length as the vase for support. Add water.

**2.** Create the overall structure and height by installing the tall, more woody stems first, keeping them evenly spaced and vertical. I like to taper each end side with a bit more downward flow.

**3.** Fill the base of the vase loosely but thoroughly with pine needle clusters. I used white pine, which has softer, shorter needles than those of yellow or loblolly pine, but it's also easy to trim those down in order to create a grassy look.

**4.** Add the lowest part of the spectrum that you have already laid out. Consider the visual weight of various flowers and keep them low.

**5.** Finish with the middle part of the arrangement, adding lighter stems and vines in this area.

***Note:*** If you want to make a lower centerpiece, keep the branching stems as the first layer but concentrate everything closer to the base of the arrangement. Make sure it looks good on both sides by turning the vase around a couple of times as you add pieces.

# Lunar New Year

Inspiration can come from anywhere if you keep your mind open to possibilities. This design is the perfect example of that: The colors and beautiful design of a postage stamp celebrating the Chinese Lunar New Year with peach blossoms were irresistible enough for me to purchase several sheets of them for letters to both friends and garden clients. This New Year celebration just happens to be in spring, and although peaches aren't native here, related plums are and make great cut stems. Obsessed with both vintage glass vases and unusual flower frogs, I couldn't resist the chance to feature two of my latest online auction finds. The vase is low and wide, making it a challenge for arranging unless one is using floral foam (which I typically avoid due to its one-time use with fresh flowers). This beast of a flower frog was up to the task, though! Its large size and combination of metal pin and cage support make it ideal for both strong woody and soft bulb stems.

## MATERIALS

- Flowering branches of black cherry (barely open or not at all)
- Wild plum (I was drawn to the pale glow of the spent flowers)
- Dogwood
- Pinxter azalea
- Atamasco lilies

## ASSEMBLY

**1.** Fit a low, wide vase with either a big flower frog like this secured with putty, balled-up chicken wire, or floral foam held down with tape going across the top of the vase.

**2.** Create a base of flowery foliage with the black cherry stems first, placed in a wide, loose manner. They have the biggest leaves and therefore will hold the most visual green weight.

**3.** Give the vase a clockwise turn, about twenty minutes, and add some more black cherry. I chose to make a loose W shape with the left side curling toward the right like it's saying "Hi" to the right side.

**4.** Add plum branches in the same open way but situated more vertically because the stems are straight and lighter than the cherry stems.

**5.** The dogwood comes next: Stick the flowering branches just above the black cherry. Follow the same line as the black cherry, but keep the dogwood more concentrated on the left side.

**6.** Add the Pinxter azaleas next. Space them evenly toward the middle of the arrangement, mimicking the natural growth pattern, and then gradually closer together as you work down the right side.

**7.** Finally, add the Atamasco lilies in a similar manner as the azaleas but extending beyond them. This gives the effect of trumpets calling out that spring has arrived.

*Note:* Although I ultimately concentrated the design facing forward for photography purposes, it's easy to make this type of arrangement for a 360-degree view: Continue turning the vase clockwise as you work, keeping the dogwood, azaleas, and lilies in separate sections of the round.

## Coastal Plain Abundance

Signs of spring are evident as early as mid-February on the southern coastal plain, when carpets of pink moss phlox compete with the tiny jonquils that were planted generations ago. Six weeks later, as the big Gerard azalea bushes have dropped their final petals in the garden and the white flowering dogwoods have disappeared into the rapidly greening woods, the clichés of the season recede and another layer emerges. The peridot, salmon, rosy brown, and white in this piece reflect the dominant colors and tones of a spring that has sprung.

## MATERIALS

- Natives: water oak (choose stems with rosy brown tinted foliage of new growth), greybeard, itea, red maple (find branches with a rosy tint to the hanging clusters of samara), wild blueberries, pitcher plant flowers, Atamasco lilies
- Foraged non-native: sheep sorrel

## ASSEMBLY

**1.** Begin by creating a foliage base with the rosy new growth of water oak. Here they are set in a low compote vase that has a metal cage frog attached with floral putty. I like using this type of cage for woody stems.

**2.** Add the greybeard, set slightly above the oak foliage in a loose, open V pattern.

**3.** Place stems of itea as the highest element and to balance the white of the greybeard.

**4.** Set in rosy-colored maple branches so that they create an opening somewhat like a low, open vortex—ready to suck in the alien-looking pitcher plant flowers when they come around.

**5.** Add several stems of rosy-colored sheep sorrel to balance the maple's tone and add softness to the upper reaches of the composition.

**6.** Wild blueberry stems, whose fruit is not ripe but are tinged with rose from the spring sunlight, add their small, rounded texture for interest and surprise.

**7.** Cluster a few pitcher plant flowers low in the vase and leave another one tall, like it is saying "Hi" to passing neighbors.

# Brownie Points

Chocolate-colored foliage and flowers are fairly uncommon and therefore steal the show when used in floral design. The depth they provide both draws the eye in and gives the lighter components something to bounce off of. Over the last several years, there has been a boom in baptisia breeding that has produced nativars in not only a wide range of colors but also plant sizes, from purple-flowered varieties that can reach 4 or 5 feet down to a pink one that is only about 2 feet tall.

**MATERIALS**

- Burgundy ninebark (*Physocarpus* 'Coppertina')
- Baptisia 'Brownie Points,' 'Cherries Jubilee,' and 'Carolina Moonlight' flowers and foliage
- Golden alexander (zizia) or other yellow, umbel-shaped flower like dill
- Mock orange (*Philadelphius*)
- Locust flowers

## ASSEMBLY

**1.** Use floral putty to attach a small (1-inch) pin frog to the bottom of a stemmed vase no bigger than a wine cup. I used vintage milk glass.

**2.** Choose three ninebark branches with good horizontal angles and set in the pin frog at angles to replicate the natural growth of the plant.

**3.** Add dark baptisia flowers, mimicking the direction of the ninebark but slightly closer together.

**4.** Add more baptisia, then begin to place the golden alexander, which will hover at the top of the arrangement—like dancing fireflies.

**5.** Add blue-green baptisia foliage for fullness and continue with a few more baptisia and golden alexander flowers. I also added a couple stems of invasive Japanese spirea (the rosy-brown foliage caught my eye). Maple foliage would be nice too.

**6.** Add mock orange flower stems, tucking them in close to the center of the arrangement.

**7.** Add a few more mock orange stems as needed (still inside the arrangement) to distribute the white blooms evenly, and then poke in a locust branch so that the cascading sprays are lower and at the outer edge of everything else.

**8.** Finish with a few more locust flowers and make any adjustments if needed.

## Flame Azaleas and White: Large Arrangement

Flame azaleas are some of my very favorite Appalachian native cut flowers. I love the genetic diversity displayed from one plant to the next—the intensity of their yellow to orange to nearly red makes the rapidly greening hillsides far more interesting. The big trees are flowering at the same time—mostly white—but the tulip poplars, with their unique green-yellow-orange combination, add something special to native floristry this time of year.

## MATERIALS

- Natives: flame azaleas, tulip poplar, buckeye flowers (optional), black cherry (budded but not open), pagoda dogwood, false Solomon's seal, maple leaf viburnum, Solomon's seal
- Garden flowers: 'Dalmation White' foxglove

## ASSEMBLY

**1.** Gather all the materials you need to make a full arrangement. Since this piece really consists of only three colors—green, white, and orange—it's nice to present an interesting mix of foliage and flower textures and shapes. Select a tall, heavy vase that will not topple when it is full of woody branches. I started with tulip poplar and a few buckeye flowers.

**2.** Fill in with more tulip poplar to create an inner framework. As with the majority of my designs, this is not meant to be a symmetrical composition but one that reflects the natural growth of the plants themselves. Notice how the left side points at an upward tilt and the line points down as it moves to the right. Even the buds of the tulip poplar in the center are situated to move

in that direction. As the design progresses, the orientation will actually flip directions, thus giving the entire piece a natural sense of movement.

**3.** Add branches of black cherry blossoms so that their long clusters fill in and create light movement in the upper reaches of the composition.

**4.** Add the flame azalea branches that have bigger flowers and a more open framework first, so they circle the general outline of the arrangement.

**5.** Add an azalea branch with a beautiful cascading habit, and fill in with ivory plumes of false Solomon's seal throughout the piece. Don't forget to turn the vase as you go to avoid a one-sided final outcome.

**6.** Create a focal point by clustering maple leaf viburnum, with its white, umbel-shaped flower clusters, low in the center. A branch or two of pagoda dogwood, with similar, less advanced flowers, balances those in the upper reaches, and a single flourish of a tall Solomon's seal stem sprouts from the top.

**7.** Finally, add the tallest branch of azalea, still in bud. The flowers will gradually open, making the entire piece unfold every day, just like the surrounding forest. I added several stems of white foxglove from the garden, too, because I love the way they twist and bend as the flowers open over a week or two.

# SUMMER TUTORIALS

FLORAL DESIGN THIS TIME OF YEAR may feel daunting—days are hotter, more humid, and the nights don't cool down much. Swimming pools, cocktails, and the tree frog soundtrack of nights outside on the porch are our only relief. The holidays that come and go in the three months officially designated as "summer" are milestones on the calendar to tell us what time of year it is. With the exception of the mountains, humidity is a near constant, and once April rolls around, temps start to hit the 80s on a regular basis, creep to the 90s by early June, and often don't go back down until late October. Our native plants, however, manage to keep us on track with their production of flowers and fruit on a fairly predictable schedule. Grace your life with the abundance of both this season.

## Garden Party: Summer Fruits and Local Pottery

As the heart of summer approaches, woody plants begin to give way from spring blossoms to green berries to the sweetness of the earlier fruits like raspberries, cherries, and blueberries. It is certainly warm outside but not sweltering, making it a great time for a garden party. No need to be fancy, but why not use the good stuff when you set the table for a lovely evening? Invest in a set of low vases from a local potter—they bring an added sense of place to centerpieces and keep things from being pretentious. Clip simple stems from the garden, throw something on the grill, toss a salad, wrap something sweet into a quick tart, light the candles, and sit back and enjoy your friends as the light fades and the fireflies come out. Maybe put some jazz on while you do it all . . .

### MATERIALS
- Natives: blueberry, cherry, raspberry, blackberry, raspberry fruits and foliage; sourwood foliage
- Garden flowers: sea holly and early phlox

## ASSEMBLY

**1.** Throw a simple cover on the table. I used a big piece of linen I dyed (the edges aren't even finished). Set the table and space the water-filled vases evenly along its length.

**2.** Begin with a base of light-shaded foliage and then distribute the berries evenly in each vase. I chose black raspberry leaves and berries plus green blueberries.

**3.** Tuck in stems with richer tones for contrast, but keep it loose. Cherries and the fresh rosy growth of sour-wood leaves were used here.

**4.** Add a few more stems of flowers that complement the soft-toned foliage you added first. Phlox and sea holly were easy choices here, but you should grab whatever is close at hand and looks good.

**5.** If you still have some stems left, fill out the vases with them or scatter them on the table around the vases.

**6.** Step back, straighten what needs to be straightened, and go finish that salad or tart!

# Butterfly Milkweed Mix

This design is a good example of how powerful your choice of foliage can be. I am drawn to chartreuse foliage like a moth is to a lightbulb. It brings light to arrangements and accents most other colors in floral design. It does the same in the garden by brightening shady spots and serving as a brilliant backdrop to other flowers, foliage, and berries. I have a rather eclectic collection in my garden, and I add more selections every year—from annuals to trees.

This color may occur in foliage as random genetic sports and seedlings or be a sign of a stressed plant. I have seen large oak trees throw out entire branches covered in leaves this color, shining like a beacon among the deep greens of summer, and wondered how I could get to them. The foliage used in this design was actually within reach—foraged from the roadside. There might not have been adequate nutrients for the little tree, or maybe it was a reaction to runoff roadside salt. Either way, it was good snag!

## MATERIALS

- Natives: chlorotic white oak foliage, trumpet vine flowers, butterfly milkweed, thimbleberry flowers, jersey tea
- Nativars: apricot yarrow ('Summer Pastels' selection), echinacea 'Cheyenne Spirit'
- Garden flowers: *Astilbe taquettii*

## ASSEMBLY

**1.** Select a small, footed vase (this one is about 6 inches tall and 4 inches wide) and secure a pin frog to the bottom with floral putty.

**2.** Fill the vase with the oak foliage in a full organic shape, securing the stems in the frog. I cut longer pieces down and used about six stems.

**3.** Strip the trumpet vine foliage and add the flower stems following the general directions of the oak.

**4.** Adjust the trumpet vine as necessary and add the first piece of milkweed—it is a visual base to begin with.

**5.** Add more milkweed, loosely distributing it throughout the foliage, not forgetting the back side of the foliage.

**6.** Add the thimbleberry flowers or another small, rounded, bright pink flower. I placed it here so that it formed a diagonal line from the bottom left to the top right.

**7.** Add some yarrow, keeping it loose and fairly low in the composition to soften the colors just a bit. I also added some white jersey tea flowers, placing them so they are the same length as the oak along the higher curve of the outline.

**8.** Finally, add the echinacea and astilbe.

## Pennycress Wreath

A fresh wreath adorning a door or wall is a welcome sight in any season. Choosing materials that hold up to the door opening and closing, and age gracefully, and wrapping them on the frame in a sturdy manner are the keys to success. The following steps can be applied again and again throughout the year with an array of materials. Dogwood branches in early spring when the flowers are still very tight, magnolia in summer, goldenrod or rabbit tobacco in fall, and juniper, waxmyrtle, pine, and holly in winter are all great choices that can be mixed or used alone. Consider embellishing with any other material that has interesting texture and color. Sumac berries, pitcher plant trumpets, feathers, flowering grasses, and rose hips are just a few that come to mind.

Pennycress is a fun and easy material to work with, as it is easily found in large numbers and readily transitions through several seasons as it ages. I love giving it a light coating of metallic copper craft spray for some tongue-in-cheek holiday bling (copper "penny"cress). Although you can purchase metal wreath frames, grapevine is usually abundant wherever there is a wild spot, and you don't need much—just enough to wrap it around itself two or three times to make a light but sturdy circle. I prefer to use a roll of floral wire because it is easily held, but alternatively you may choose a flat paddle of wire (not comfortable in my hands).

## MATERIALS
- Grapevine, about 4 feet wrapped into a circle about 12 inches in diameter
- Pennycress, thirty-six to forty-eight pieces about 12 inches long, cut while still green (I used thirty-six, but it's always good to have backups)
- Floral wire (between 20 and 24 gauge works best)

## ASSEMBLY
**1.** Lay out twelve piles of the penny-cress. Laying out bunches is a helpful way to make sure your material is evenly distributed—that way you don't run out before you reach the end. I also use this method when making mixed-material wreaths; you can design your pattern and make changes *before* you are in the middle of assembly.

As a rule of thumb, anticipate about one bunch for every inch of diameter that your wreath frame is (if you are using a 20-inch frame, you'll need twenty bunches). Also note that while bunch length (9 to 12 inches) is about the same for wreaths between 12 and 16 inches in diameter, they will need to be longer and fuller as you go up in size, to create a full-looking wreath of this style.

**2.** Attach the wire to the frame by wrapping it around once and then twisting the end part of the wire back onto the main part of the wire several times so that it is tight and doesn't come loose. ***Note:*** Since this is a simple wreath, I condensed my pennycress bunches into four piles by stacking the individual bunches in alternating directions so that they are easy to reach as I work.

**3.** Attach the first bunch to the frame by laying it on top where the wire is twisted on. Position the bunch so that the stems are running evenly with the frame at that point; envision a circle sitting on a line— that is where you situate bunches each time as you go around the entire frame. You don't want the stems to be pointing drastically into the center of the circle, nor the fluffy ends—just follow the line.

**4.** Wrap the wire around the bunch and the frame two or three times, moving down the frame as you go— not in just one place.

**5.** Lay the next bunch on and make sure that it is spaced in a way that the fluffy end makes a continuous flow of green from the first bunch. Too close together and you get a big fat pile, too far apart and the wreath will not have a continuously round outer edge. Wrap the wire around two to three more times as in Step 4 and trim the stems.

**6.** Give stems that are excessively long a trim.

**7.** Once you've positioned the third bunch, lean back from the wreath and double-check your spacing. You've placed 25 percent of the bunches at this point. Have you covered 25 percent of the frame? This is the time to correct your spacing if necessary—*before* you wrap that third bunch on. Good to go? Wrap that bunch on and continue adding and wrapping on bunches.

**8.** This is what it should look like halfway through. You can fluff and adjust as you go or do that at the end.

**9.** This is what the wreath looks like when you have two bunches left to add. If the space where my hand is in this picture is any wider, you'll need a thirteenth bunch. If the space is a lot narrower, consider adding just one more bunch.

**10.** Time to add the final bunch. The last one is the hardest to get in there evenly. This is another reason using fresh, flexible materials that will dry is easier than using more-brittle already dried materials.

**11.** Lift up the very first bunch that was added. Again, using fresh materials means less breakage at the end step.

**12.** Carefully slide the last bunch end under the first bunch, making sure that it is evenly spaced like the others (you may have to trim the bunch down a little if it sticks out more than usual). Wrap the wire around once to secure it in place.

**13.** Once the bunch is secured, unroll the wire so you have about a 12-inch length and cut it from the roll with a pair of wire cutters. (Don't be silly like me and use your pruners—that really isn't what they are made for.)

**14.** With your fingers, make a 1- to 2-inch loop right where the Step 12 wrap was made, close to the wreath frame, and then wrap the length of the wire tail around the frame and bunch one more time.

**15.** Once you've gone around the frame with the wire and everything feels secure, wrap the tail of the wire several times around the base of the loop you made. If there is still loose wire, you can either trim it or wrap it around the frame until there is no more.

**16.** Voila! This is what the wreath looks like right after you finish it. That nifty loop you made to end the wrapping is the perfect way to hang your wreath on a nail or hook.

**17.** Pennycress ages gracefully to a lovely golden color in a couple of weeks and will look pretty for up to a year if hung in a well-ventilated spot and kept dry.

**18.** If you want to bling your wreath out for the holidays, break out the metallic craft spray. As I mentioned, I love the copper for this particular material, but gold or silver looks lovely too.

**19.** A copper pennycress wreath ready to go the distance. The paint may add another year to its life span, but you still have to keep it dry.

# Red, White, and Blue

I grew up picking blackberries to snack on and make jam with my sister every summer. My mother would make us put on long sleeves and jeans in the sweltering Georgia heat so that we wouldn't get any redbugs while we were in the brambles. It was worth it, though, and the tradition continues with my nieces. The only difference is that here in the mountains, we don't have redbugs, so we can pick away wearing shorts!

Blackberries and oakleaf hydrangeas come into their own around Independence Day, and I can't think of a better way to celebrate that special day than to decorate with our native fruits and berries. This arrangement can be done any time after the hydrangeas have hardened off a bit (so they don't droop) and the brambles are loaded with fruit.

## MATERIALS

- Natives: blackberry branches—select arching pieces that are loaded with ripe and unripe berries and cut 24 inches long (leather gloves are recommended when harvesting); midsummer aster or any airy little white daisy

- Nativar: oakleaf hydrangeas (I used the double-flowered 'Snowflake' cultivar, which just happens to be growing in my mountain garden)

- Queen Anne's lace (not native, but definitely foraged)

## ASSEMBLY

**1.** Select a tall, narrow vase that has some weight to it—berry branches are heavy and can topple light containers. You don't need extra support inside the vase if it has a narrow opening, but a ball of chicken wire can be used if it makes you feel better about things.

**2.** Begin by placing several shorter blackberry stems in the vase. I used stems I had cut from the longer branches that made an upside-down L shape. This provides a good base to support the big, arching blackberry stems. If you filled the container with a ball of chicken wire for support, you can skip this step.

**3.** Add the long blackberry stems, positioning them so they arch away from the center and are spaced evenly from one another. I like to have them fall at varying heights. This gives the entire arrangement a loose, natural feeling rather than a stiffly contrived one.

**4.** Position three hydrangeas so that they casually follow the lines of the blackberry stems without repeating them exactly.

**5.** Continue to add a few more hydrangeas until you are satisfied with the balance between them and the blackberries.

**6.** Stick in a handful of tall Queen Anne's lace stems so that they hover lightly above the main profile of the composition.

**7.** Finally add the airy little summer daisies. These tall but unobtrusive annuals smell incredible and bring a little yellow-eyed twinkle to the arrangement. Stems of airy, yellow-rayed flowers would be another great option if you can't find any white ones.

# Fascinator Demo

Proof that you can make just about anything pretty with some chicken wire and zip ties! I call this design a "fascinator," because the way it can perch on the corner of a door frame, window, or arbor reminds me of the headpieces that British ladies of a certain class are known to wear on special occasions. Just think of me as your hillbilly Phillip Treacy guru and let your imagination run wild with the possibilities. The way I roll the chicken wire and hang it creates a good structure in which the stems are secure (floral foam is not absolutely necessary for this design). It will, however, take some trial and error on your part to see what materials hold up the best for the amount of time you need them to, which will vary by season. If you are eschewing the foam, consider adding a balled-up piece of the chicken wire in its place for extra sticking power.

## MATERIALS

- Natives: black tupelo foliage, lime-green oak foliage, sourwood, rhododendron (or magnolia), mountain mint, trumpet vine, smilax vine, Turk's cap lilies, yarrow
- Garden flowers and foliage: flowering dill heads, zinnias, lilium 'Lady Alice,' nicotiana 'Giant Lime,' weigela
- Zip ties or very long nails (depending on what your base is)
- Chicken wire
- Floral foam
- Ladder (and a helper to hold the ladder for safety)

## ASSEMBLY

Either before or after you have gathered all of the beautiful plant materials you want to use, there are a few tasks before the fun design part begins:

**1.** Get two big blocks (or one sliced in half length-wise) of floral foam soaking in some warm water.

**2.** While that is happening, cut two large rectangles of chicken wire with a pair of metal shears or wire cutters.

**3.** When the foam is saturated, wrap it up length-wise in the chicken wire and bend the wire edges around the other side to secure it. This can't be too tight, or you will needlessly cut into the foam (contact edges can also be protected with a double layer of wax paper). One other drop of wisdom: If you are doing this installation for an event, hang the wired foam where it needs to be long enough in advance that any excess water drips and evaporates before there are people in nice clothes hanging out underneath. A little extra drink of water can always be added with a spouted watering can if needed.

**4.** Attach the chicken wire cages to your chosen framework. Since I am working around a door frame for this series, I used two long nails for each cage, securing them at the top. For an arbor, they are easily secured with big zip ties.

**5a.** Begin adding your plant material—first with a base of foliage that outlines the main silhouette of the design (I chose weigela), and then start to fill in with another variety.

**5b.** I chose this bright (chlorotic) green oak because I liked the contrast of shape and the accenting color.

**6.** Flowering rhododendron branches add a visual heft with their foliage as well as sturdy flowers. Southern magnolia would be a good substitute. If you want to add any other foliage, this is a good time to do it—before most of the flowers go in. I love using sourwood foliage and anything variegated I can find.

**7.** Cooling silvery mountain mint is tucked in here and there, and the bright orange flowers of trumpet vine and Turk's cap lilies are loosely distributed throughout the piece.

**8a.** When it comes to pieces like this, I want them to look as though they might be wild themselves—a re-creation of something found hanging from an overgrown fence or sprouting out of the crook of an ancient tree. The most natural way to achieve this is by adding the long tips of vines.

**8b.** Stick pieces in so they are crawling across the top of your framework and trailing down the bottom. Add one or two small tack nails at an upward angle to perch the upper vine on so it doesn't droop over the doorway.

**9.** Add peachy-colored lilies and yarrow next. Continue to maintain a loose distribution of your materials in order to keep it looking wild and natural.

**10.** This is the part when you stand back and take in your work. You could stop now or keep going. I am a maximalist and so I kept going . . .

**11.** The faces of garden zinnias in complementary colors bring more personality to the mix, and for a highlight, giant yet airy flowering dill heads are situated deep in the arrangement and green nicotiana accents the outskirts of the piece.

**12.** Stand back one more time and make any final adjustments. I added one more piece of the smilax vine at the bottom to make it flow and grow even more.

## Lavender and Peach

In this arrangement, I show how natives can serve as the base in a pastel spectrum. From the icy cool lavenders of mountain mint and wild bergamot to the warmly blushed sourwood is a bridge of purple liatris and red-eyed lavender phlox. Whenever I am doing an arrangement like this, I find it very helpful to first lay out all the materials in the spectrum I want. I might not use everything I've laid out, and sometimes something else is needed as the assembly progresses. In this instance, the peachy-cream spikes of plume poppy were the "extra little sumthin'" on the peach side that I needed. Other possible last-minute fill-ins could be the dried straw shades of pennycress or the foxtail heads of grass flowers. Purple zinnias can easily substitute for the dahlias. As a final flourish, sweetly scented species of lilies were added. The balance struck by their upwardly curved petals and downwardly hanging stamens brings an actively opening, different shape to the composition.

### MATERIALS

- Natives: mountain mint, sourwood, *Monarda fistulosa*, *Phlox pillosa*, liatris
- Garden flowers: plume poppy; phlox 'Cherry Caramel' and 'Crème Brulee'; dahlias 'Koko Puff,' 'Sir Richard,' and 'Valley Tawny'; zinnias 'Queen Red Lime,' 'Zinderella Peach,' 'Isabellina,' and 'Queen Coral'; snapdragon 'Opus Lavender'; lilium 'Lady Alice'; and *Lilium lankongense*

## ASSEMBLY

**1.** Attach a pin or cage frog to the bottom of a small vase. I chose a hobnail milk glass vase with a simple cup shape about 4 inches tall. Fill two-thirds with water.

**2.** Place the mountain mint and sourwood at opposite sides of the vase, securing well into the frog. Make sure that each goes about halfway around the vase for a 360-degree arrangement.

**3.** Add about three stems each of monarda and plume poppy. You want these blooms to be at the outer edges or beyond the foliage. If they are too short, they will get lost as other materials are added.

**4.** Add all of the phlox—native and non-native—so that the flowers are just below the frame of foliage, keeping with the cool to warm shading.

**5.** Spiky purple liatris comes next. These need to be the tallest element in the arrangement and should balance out the other stems already in place.

**6.** Fill in the lower part of the cool side with the purple flowers, keeping the smallest blooms higher and progressing the colors accordingly.

**7.** Add the 'Queen Red Lime' zinnias next, keeping them low and close to the purple flowers added in Step 6.

**8.** Add the 'Zinderella Peach' zinnias. These can be higher than the other round flowers from Steps 6 and 7 because the color is lighter and they carry the eye upward.

**9.** Step back and make any adjustments you see fit. I moved one of the Queen zinnias lower, and added a buff-colored dahlia and lavender snapdragon.

**10.** Lilium 'Lady Alice' is added to the warm side and allowed to hang just beyond the foliage. If you are using lilies that are different colors, place according to the color scheme or leave them out entirely.

**11.** Lavender-flowered *Lilium lankongense* is placed high with the liatris since it has smaller flowers. I also moved one of the 'Queen Red Lime' zinnias because it felt too heavy. That's the advantage of working with metal frogs rather than floral foam—it's fine to move things around without compromising the integrity of the support structure.

**12.** Give the vase a spin and view it from above. If there are any holes to fill in or placement you aren't satisfied with, make adjustments. I added more zinnias, peach lilies, and a dahlia for fun.

## Maypop Blue and Cool Pink in a Compote

Since I live in the mountains, passionflowers—"maypops" are hard to come by until later in the season, and I had one single bloom for this demo. I wanted to make the most of that special flower and bring the cool blues and sweet pinks to a small arrangement. Cosmos are easy-to-grow annuals that love hot, sunny conditions. I finally got around to trying the newer garden variety 'Cupcakes,' and I am in love with the pleated petals that resemble paper cupcake wrappers.

### MATERIALS
- Natives: maypop vine with flowers and buds, *Verbena hastata*, ageratum (*Conoclinum*), blue lobelia, *Phlox pillosa*
- Garden flowers: cosmos 'Cupcakes,' dahlia 'Jasmine Pearl'

## ASSEMBLY

**1.** Select a small vase and secure a small, round pin frog in the center. I used an amber compote with an iridescent finish to complement the background rust, bring out the hints of red in the maypop and phlox flowers' centers, and give the overall design more depth.

**2.** First, secure the verbena around the outer edges of the vase. Although it is a spiky filler, I keep it low here in anticipation of adding the spikier lobelia in Step 6.

**3.** Add the maypop vine. I cut mine in half to add extra vine movement and set the accent flower, allowing it to naturally hang the way it was growing. This makes for a less forced composition.

**4.** Fluffy blue ageratum is next. Position it in a loose manner but keeping somewhat close to the rim of the vase. It is the textural color answer to the verbena hovering above.

**5.** Stick in some short stems of phlox, going all the way around the vase's circumference.

**6.** Insert the blue lobelia in an evenly spaced manner so that it defines the top of the composition in a low, rounded manner.

**7.** Bunch six to nine open stems of cosmos (save your biggest blooms for Step 8) in your hand so that they all top out at about the same height. Cut them all at once at a height where they will hover above the phlox, and then place them together in the pin frog. Allow them to flop the way they want to go. You can adjust later.

**8.** Fill in with your remaining big flowers. Let some spill over the vase and tuck in a couple closer to the rim. I added a single pale lavender waterlily dahlia ('Jasmine Pearl') at a 90-degree angle from the may-pop stems' point of origin. Fluff and adjust to your liking, don't fret over it, and enjoy!

# Parallel Universes: A Tale of Two Colors

I thought it would be cool to demonstrate the power of color choices while at the same time reinforcing the premise that good form can be interpreted in many ways. What better way to do that than beginning with a common base and then simultaneously repeating the assembly using two different color groups? They are not identical because Mother Nature doesn't work that way, but both the coral and the pink designs have a similar selection of stem types. For the foliage, berries, and fluffy filler, I used both native and nativar selections and then added "face" flowers of 'Queen' zinnia and 'Knock Out' rose varieties. Both are easy to grow in the Southeast, and you can pick them from your garden or buy them from your local flower farmer. Once again, it is always very helpful to first lay out your materials in a spectrum.

## MATERIALS

- Natives: American hazelnut (choose a mix of stems with nice foliage and good filbert set), ninebark, cranberry viburnum, false Solomon's seal berries, pokeweed berries with foliage stripped, monarda

- Nativars: *Hydrangea arborescens* 'Annabelle' and 'Annabelle Pink,' *Hydrangea quercifolia* 'Snowflake' and 'Alice,' ninebark 'Coppertina'
- Garden flowers: roses 'Knock Out Double Pink,' 'Knockout Coral,' 'Eden,' and 'Pretty in Pink Eden'; zinnias 'Queen Coral,' 'Queen Red Lime,' and 'Candy Mix'

## ASSEMBLY

**1.** Select a low, bowl-shaped vase and affix a cage frog with floral putty to the center.

**2.** Stick three or four hazelnut stems around the perimeter of the vase. Keep them low and fairly horizontal. Remove any extra foliage that takes away from the decorative filbert clusters.

**Coral**

**Pink**

*Throughout this section, photos on the left are coral design and those on the right are pink design.*

**3.** The hanging berries are next: false Solomon's seal in the coral mix and pokeweed berries in the pink mix, with leaves removed from the stems. Space them evenly around the vase, but the heights at which they fall should vary—just like they would if they were hanging from the plant.

**4.** Fill in gaps in the greenery with the ninebark—green for the coral and 'Coppertina' in the pink.

**5.** The first layer of hydrangeas is added next; I set them in so that one side is horizontally situated and the other side vertical—this adds more movement to the piece.

**6.** The second layer of hydrangeas, at slightly differing heights, is used to fill in the central part of the arrangement. I left space in between them to allow for the next layers and to avoid overstuffing.

**7.** Accent roses are added in groups of threes. I also slipped some cranberry viburnum into the coral design.

**8.** At this step, I only placed a couple of zinnias to get a feel for how their individual colors reacted with the roses.

**9.** Add more roses and zinnias—filling in between the rounded hydrangeas throughout the entire piece. Make sure that the whole grouping looks good when viewed from both above and all the way around.

**10.** As a flirty final touch, I added a couple of monarda stems, placing at least one of the blooms so that it extends past everything else in the vase.

# Summer Gold

As we ease into late summer, the golden-rayed flowers of native sunflowers, spikes of false foxglove, and the earliest goldenrods find a place in a few pine boughs for a simple and elegant composition. It's too hot outside to do much more.

## MATERIALS

- Natives: pine branches, and a mix of yellow flowers in varying shapes and sizes such as round "face" flowers like rudbeckia, coreopsis, and helianthus as well as some spiky selections such as solidago and false foxglove
- Garden flowers: dill heads

## ASSEMBLY

**1.** Select a low, solid-colored container. I used turquoise, but red, yellow, or cobalt would also set off the yellows and greens.

**2.** Secure a large glass flower frog to the bottom with floral putty and organize your face flowers from the smallest to the largest.

**3.** Start with pine branches, adding enough to create a full silhouette. I used white pine, which has a lighter feeling to it than some species. If the pine you are using has longer, thicker needles, set them lower and wider in the vase. If you are using pine with shorter needles that run up and down the branches more, consider making this framework more horizontal.

**4.** Next, add the stems with the smallest flowers, so that they hover just above the pine, and loosely situate those that are slightly larger throughout the equator of the greenery.

**5.** Add the tallest spiky yellow stems (false foxglove here) next, placing them to erupt loosely above everything else. Follow the general outline for continuity.

**6.** The shorter, more rounded spikes of goldenrod are added next in the lower latitudes of the arrangement.

**7.** Space large black-eyed Susans evenly throughout the central oval of the core design.

**8.** Fill in the lower part with more black-eyed Susans, giving the composition more weight and visual pop. These flowers can be more casually placed, with some closer to the center and others facing slightly downward.

**9.** Finally, add the dill heads at the top in alternating heights. Although they are larger, they are lighter in both color and visual weight. In the garden, they hover above the others and should do so here as well.

# FALL TUTORIALS

WHEREVER YOU ARE IN THE SOUTHEAST, you know when fall has arrived. The light changes almost overnight as the air sheds the weight of humidity, and everything you see is a bit clearer. It is still warm out and even downright hot if you are in the direct sun. The sun's rays may intensify the colors of certain plants while fading others, thus creating contrasts of texture, light, and color not found any other time of year. Goldenrod and asters turn roadsides and untended pastures into giant patchwork quilts of yellow, blue, and white as the bronzy panicles of grass flowers hover just above. Random "pings" are heard as acorns fall from their trees, congregating on driveways and sidewalks as Mother Nature plays her wild game of marbles. By this time, I have dropped all restraint—the field is overflowing with more dahlias than we could possibly cut and the wildflowers are beckoning nonstop. We've reached maximum capacity on pretty before it all fades into the long winter nights.

## Softly Faded Warm Tones and Airy Sky Blues

This general design is one that I find myself repeating often in the days of autumn. By now, you've figured out some of the basic methods and so I am keeping this one short—it is hard to mess up flower arrangements this time of year. I love making over-the-top giant compositions using a tall, heavy urn to hold it all together and maintain the balance both visually and physically. Display a beauty like this in front of a large window to bring the changing season closer to you. Greet guests with it in an entrance foyer on a substantial round table like Oscar de la Renta once did in his vacation home, or place in front of a mirror on a side table. Or, like me, on top of a wooden wine crate in the outdoor flower shed. Point being, you can't go wrong. Enjoy.

### MATERIALS
- Natives: Blushed sourwood foliage, goldenrod, silverrod, any aster species with blue flowers, thimbleweed (*Anemone virginiana*), seeded clematis vine, oakleaf (or panicle) hydrangea, Virginia creeper vine
- Garden flowers: Dahlias, zinnias, chrysanthemums—choose flowers of varying sizes in shades of copper, peach, terracotta, blush, ivory, and faded rose

## ASSEMBLY

**1.** Begin by laying out your native ingredients in a spectrum to see what you are working with. Do you have a good color balance? How about texture? Does it feel like anything is missing? If so, think about what you can add to bring these materials together. Conversely, if there is anything that shouts at you as not belonging, this is the time to take it out of the batch.

**2.** Since this is a big, bodacious arrangement in a tall, heavy urn, begin with a strong foliage base of sourwood. It will help hold the other stems in place and provides a backdrop that the array of muted shades can play against.

**3.** Seeded clematis vine is placed growing from the base edge. Have fun with these stems, allowing them to both climb the sourwood and cascade down the urn.

**4.** Once you have placed the clematis, situate the hydrangeas first. Then, following the outline of the greenery, fill in with the rest of the natives. Think of them floating in a meadow in autumn's afternoon sunlight. Don't forget to leave a few stems out for final adjustments after the big, round garden blooms are in.

**5.** Organize a big pile of dahlias and zinnias by size and color. There are a lot of ways you can go with these: one similar soft color in a bunch of different sizes, or a greater range of both shapes, sizes, and colors. Just make sure there aren't any that jump out and scream, that's not what this design is about!

**6.** Begin adding the "face" flowers. Don't forget to turn the urn as you go. As you can see in the photo, one of the big dahlias is way too high in the arrangement and doesn't look very comfortable. Keep those big ones low!

**7.** After you have either run out of flowers or the urn won't hold any more without risking a topple at the slightest breeze, take a step back and see how it all looks. Adjust as needed. Once you have everything in place, be sure there is water all the way to the top of the urn—that many stems will chug the water for a day or two, and you don't want any stem bases that end higher in the urn to droop from early thirst.

# Chartreuse and Purple:
# Breaking Down the Components

Early October in the longleaf forests of the coastal plain is the time when things come to life again after the long summer. The oppressive humidity subsides, reluctantly giving way to turquoise skies and longer afternoon shadows. Diminutive blooms in every color of the rainbow appear floating above the golden wiregrass. Beautyberry bushes are loaded with electric purple berries, and the intense chartreuse of tall pitcher plants stand out in the bogs. The complementary colors of these species play well together this time of year in a large centerpiece.

For this series, I took the opportunity to demonstrate the composition starting from the completed design and breaking it back down to the beginning by removing each element in the reverse order it was added. Doing this kind of breakdown on your own is an excellent way to learn more about your personal style and improve the way you put things together. Successful floral designs are composed in layers that work together to achieve a flowing, cohesive silhouette.

## MATERIALS
- Pitcher plant trumpets and flowers (*Sarracenia flava*), blazing star (*Liatris* sp.), coreopsis, hatpins, wild ageratum, beautyberry (*Callicarpa americana*), pokeweed (foliage and berries removed), titi flowers, rayless sunflowers

## ASSEMBLY

**1.** The completed centerpiece is brimming with varying shades of yellow and purple. There is an array of different textures, and the small, round white hat pins add a surprise element and play off the white vase.

**2.** The pitcher plant flowers were the last to go in, and although they brought rounded "face" flowers to the composition, they weren't necessary. As it is now, the piece is complete—not overstuffed—and it is easier to see all of the interesting smaller elements without them.

**3.** The skyrocketing liatris was next. Although the entire piece still is not lacking, the straight stems of fuzzy liatris play off the round, fuzzy ageratum.

**4.** The dancing yellow flowers of coreopsis are certainly missed now that they are gone. They brought an airy texture that made it all feel wild and free. And no more hat pins to visually tie the white vase to the materials.

**5.** With the soft ageratum gone, everything seems hard and pointy to an extreme. Their color, being more of a bluish purple, softened the more striking tones in there.

**6.** Goodness gracious! Now that the beautyberry stems are out, it looks like someone cranked the top off a jack-in-the-box full of bellowing Dr. Seuss–style trumpets.

**7.** Things just got a lot quieter. The trumpets remaining are on the skinny side and they were originally added to establish a vertical line. Notice the Florida anise at the base on the right side? Its star-shaped seedpods were completely lost when it was all done and should have been saved for another arrangement where they could be appreciated.

**8.** The pokeweed stems are highly visible now and form an open V framework. I love using the brilliant stems, and, quite frankly, these were too short. They would have done the job I intended if they were able to form the same framework *above* the trumpets, not below them. Unfortunately, the winds of Hurricane Mike made quick work of most of them right before I got there.

**9.** Finally, the swamp cyrilla (or titi) stems. I loved their cascading clusters and thought they worked well visually flowing out of the container. That said, those small, round seed capsules shed like crazy, and I will not use this plant again at this stage. I have not tested it at the flowering stage—it may be a true winner then—and it isn't included in the plant guide. But as I have mentioned before, most things are worth trying!

**10.** Back at the normal Step 1: materials laid out, a ball of chicken wire support in the vase—but with lessons learned (at least for me).

**11.** I must mention the container! Borrowed from my mother's pantry full of vases and planters, it has probably held more potted African violets than floral centerpieces, but I think it's perfect. Pieces like this are worth seeking out in vintage and antiques stores!

# Persimmons and Dahlias

The fruits of the persimmon tree begin to ripen in September and October, right about the time dahlias peak. The foliage can be five different colors at once, and I like to echo the purple tones with beautyberry branches. From a design perspective, there isn't a thing I don't like about persimmons. They are also excellent in their cool, light green form earlier in the season. Just remember—those fruits look yummy, but wait to taste until they are about to fall off the branch!

## MATERIALS

- Natives: fruited persimmon branches, sourwood foliage, goldenrod, beautyberry stems, panicum grass flowers
- Garden flowers: warm-toned dahlias of varying sizes, *Mina lobata* 'Exotic Love Vine,' yellow garden mums, coleus

## ASSEMBLY

**1.** Choose a sturdy vase with warm colors that complement the materials you are using. I used a vintage amber glass vase with a long stem, but a small bowl will also work. Secure a cage/pin frog to the bottom with floral putty.

**2.** Stick about four persimmon branches into the frog; they are heavy with fruit, so make sure you get them in there securely. I like to have them casually flop out of the vase, so that they look like they did when they were on the tree. Make the most of the foliage that is particularly colorful and trim any unsightly leaves off.

**3.** Add a couple of sourwood stems (or more persimmon) to fill in a bit more. I also added a piece of coleus with a purple underside for more contrast with the fruit.

**4.** Situate the largest dahlias so they casually radiate down low in the vase. Big flowers have visual weight and don't need to fly high.

**5.** Incorporate a selection of smaller "face" flowers that echo the bigger flowers in shape and color, but place them slightly higher in the outline.

**6.** Add a spiky element with goldenrod, radiating it upward from the longest horizontal persimmon branch. I always like to use groups of three when I make a move like this.

**7.** Loop in vine stems and accent open spots with shorter pieces of the downward-pointing blooms for a bit of cascading drippy-ness.

**8.** Purple beautyberry branches are added on the right to balance the solidago, and a few tall stems of airy grass plumes echo the shading of the beautyberry, sourwood, and persimmon branches' woody stems (I also like the way they wiggle).

**9.** Since this particular arrangement will be displayed on a table against a wall, I added one more stem of sourwood on the back side—mainly because the color was a perfect counter to some of the persimmon foliage hanging in the front. The overall effect is one of balance.

# Late Autumn Spectrum

The colors of late autumn are almost too much to bear in their beauty. It is as if every bloom and leaf still standing is determined to put on the show of their life before taking a long rest. Moving through this seasonal kaleidoscope is the inspiration for this arrangement. Branches of maple and tupelo provide both the architecture and the spectral base, and if placed just so may stand alone. I elaborated with several layers of native berries and flowers, then took it to another level with garden-grown vines, dahlias, and celosia. At this point in the season, expect ratty foliage, imperfect flowers, and general dishevelment—that is part of the charm. Exuberant—check. Overstuffed—probably. Should you worry about those things? Not so much. It is about all that and a box of chocolate (foliage). The end of the growing season should be celebrated by going out with a bang.

## MATERIALS

- Natives: maple, sassafras, tupelo, ninebark, beautyberry, pitcher plant trumpets, coreopsis, liatris, solidago, echinacea, rudbeckia
- Garden stems: forsythia, Rex begonia vine (*Cissus discolor*), Spanish flag vine (*Mina lobata*), silky milkweed (*Aeclepias curvassica*), zinnias, dahlias, plume celosia (optional)

## ASSEMBLY

**1.** Begin with a base of seasonal foliage. This provides structure and begins the color story.

**2.** Use more foliage with varying shapes to elaborate structure and shading.

**3.** Reinforce the base with interesting textures like berries and trumpets, and give it a little bit of movement with a funky vine.

**4.** *You can stop here*—because it is already awesome. Just make sure you have pulled together all of the elements thus far with a strong color story. Otherwise, it could be a hot mess, but I know you have been paying attention.

**5.** If you are ready to get serious, begin to fill in with airy native flowers, maintaining and accenting the existing color base.

**6.** Pop in some surprise accents like Spanish flag vine and silky milkweed.

**7.** Give the base of the piece the gravity it needs with echinacea, coneheads, and "face" flowers like rudbeckia, zinnias, and dahlias.

**8.** I also added a bit of plume celosia that I grew as an interesting vertical accent on the left side. Celosia flowers endure for weeks after a frost if you cut them, strip the leaves, and keep them from direct freezes (don't put them in a cooler).

The dahlias went in because I had to empty my walk-in cooler. I hate to see it all go and am glad I was able to use the rainbow of colors that were still hanging on.

# Dried Things: A Rabbit Tobacco Wreath

When the rabbit tobacco makes itself evident in the fall, I head out and gather some of the prettiest, bring it home, and hang it in bunches in my greenhouse to dry for later use. This wreath has a much tighter form than most of the wreaths I make because dried materials are brittle. Keeping the materials closer to the framework of the wreath makes it more durable, but more airy materials can be added once the main part of the wreath is finished—and can occasionally be refreshed as the need arrives.

## MATERIALS

- Natives: Dried rabbit tobacco, smooth sumac heads, waxmyrtle, dried pitcher plant flowers and trumpets, dried liatris

- Non-native: jimson weed pods from a neighbor's pasture. I spray-painted these pods gold. **Note:** These are highly toxic plants if ingested but are safe for floral design. Although they aren't difficult to remove, be mindful of where the seeds fall if you don't want them growing in your garden.

- Optional additions: mini ears of Indian corn, Japanese beautyberry, dried gomphrena, sorghum, Chinese lantern

## ASSEMBLY

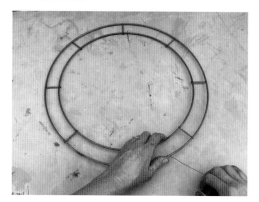

**1.** Begin by securing the end of a roll of floral wire to a metal wreath frame. Using a frame as pictured, with a double ring, provides a more stable base for bunches of dried materials.

**2.** Add the first bundle of rabbit tobacco, situating it so that it follows the curve of the frame. If it is pointed too far toward the center or out away from the frame, it will be unstable.

**3.** The next bunch is added in the same way but with a small branch of waxmyrtle on the bottom of the bunch.

**4.** Several stems of other dried materials with various shapes—pitcher plant flowers, liatris, and hat pins here—are selected and trimmed down to proportion.

**5.** Wrap the dried stems carefully so they do not break from the pressure of the wire. The rabbit tobacco does provide a bit of a cushion for these leaner stems to rest on.

**6.** Another bunch of rabbit tobacco is added and then a sumac stem is placed on top of that, wrapped and the stem trimmed.

**7.** Another bunch of rabbit tobacco is added and then more waxmyrtle, repeating the pattern begun in Steps 2 and 3.

**8.** Continue working around the wreath, adding more rabbit tobacco and other dried flowers as you go. Make sure that you are maintaining balance with the placement of the rabbit tobacco. Unlike fresh materials with more natural movement, dense, dried bundles can start to look wonky if you don't pay attention.

**9.** More sumac is added to the mix. Note that this dense head of berries can throw off the whole design if their natural form—either curving at the tip or very straight—isn't taken into consideration when placed and secured. They too can be brittle, and so adjustment at the end can be difficult.

**10.** Once you have gone about three-quarters of the way, step back and see what it looks like. Does it need something?

**11.** To make this particular wreath more interesting, it definitely needed some added flair. The seedpods of jimson weed were quickly given a light spray of plant-friendly gold paint and added. These stems are kept longer as a way of creating a focal point.

**12.** Carefully ease in the last bundle with the jimson weed and remember—if you pull back that first bundle top too far to get the last one in, those brittle stems could break!

**13.** Secure the last bunch with a few wraps of the wire. Lifting the entire piece for a better view is *very* helpful at this stage.

**14.** To finish, cut the wire, leaving about 12 inches to work with. Make a loop, wrap the wire around the frame one more time, and wrap the excess wire around the base of the loop as many times as you need to.

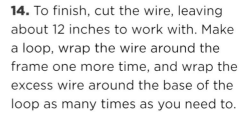

**15.** Make any necessary final adjustments with care. I usually need to shift that last bunch farther toward the center so that it lines up with the rest of the materials. You don't want it to look unstable.

**16.** There you are! A finished dried wreath that will last for up to three years if hung in a protected, dry area.

# WINTER TUTORIALS

DEPENDING ON LOCATION, winter means different things for those of us in the Southeast. Yes, the days are shorter for all of us and the nights cooler. But, while those of you in the southern coastal plain start to see signs of spring in February, around the time of Imbolc (the halfway mark between winter solstice and spring equinox), folks in the mountains continue to experience snow and freezing temps regularly all the way into late March or later. Those short days and long nights invite time to reflect, relax, and enjoy friends and family. This is the time to bring the outdoors closer as plans are made for the coming months. Evergreens and berries adorn our porches and come inside for the holidays, and branches can be cut and brought inside to force blooms, hastening spring—at least in a vase.

## Berries, Foliage, and Flowers of Winter

When early December rolls around and the bright autumn leaves have all fallen, the natural world may look a little drab. Look more closely though. You may find witch-hazel in full bloom and communities of eastern red cedar laden with shining berries, both more noticeable now that the sun hovers lower in the horizon. If there's been a freeze or two, the coralberry and smilax foliage has finally given up and their defoliated stems reveal electric pink and navy-blue berries in abundance. The following composition makes the most of four simple ingredients. Restraint and a "less is more" attitude allow each species to play an important part in this small arrangement. Display a work like this in a bright white room or set against a dark background as shown.

### MATERIALS

- Coralberry, witch-hazel, smilax, eastern red cedar

## ASSEMBLY

**1.** Select a small, solid-colored vase—preferably with a stem. I chose a vintage milk glass piece that is 6 inches high and a little under 4 inches at the mouth. Anchor a small glass or ceramic frog inside with floral putty. This type of support, with round holes, is great for woody stems.

**2.** Place two or three branches of witch-hazel in the vase so they form a V shape. Notice that overall visual balance is achieved with the proportions: one-third vase height to two-thirds stem height from the lip of the vase to the top of the branch. This rule of thumb can be applied successfully to any floral design.

**3.** Add another branch or two of witch-hazel to achieve a rounded open V. One or two stems of smilax can go in now, too. Using the tendrils of the smilax, attach the tallest one to the witch-hazel so that it hovers just below it.

**4.** Fill in with coralberry stems that are about half the height of the witch-hazel. Allow the floppier pieces to hang low and spill out of the vase.

**5.** Complete the composition with several lightweight tips of cedar, situating it below the coralberry and letting some flop out at the base where the coralberry does not.

If you desire a fuller arrangement, add another branch of taller coralberry whose clusters of berries spring out at different intervals.

## MAGNOLIA AND CEDAR WREATH

Magnolia wreaths are timeless beauties. In my opinion, with our ample supply of its beautiful foliage in the Southeast, there is no excuse to have anything but the real deal. I've made *hundreds* of magnolia wreaths since 2009. In fact, if you do a quick search on Pinterest for "fresh magnolia wreath," a photo of one of the first ones I made that year pops up—posted by Etsy . . . still. (All sold out, by the way.) Why? Because my original design is unique. It isn't heavy or hard looking as some can be, and I've always liked to incorporate other foraged materials that accent and play off the foliage. Some might say there is a bit of whimsy to them (whatever that means . . . perhaps if I attached a bunch of baby Jesus ornaments to the final product á la Daryl Hannah's creation in *Steel Magnolias*?). Anyway, y'all are getting a full tutorial on how I make a fresh green magnolia wreath. Embellish yours as you see fit!

## MATERIALS

- Natives: southern magnolia, eastern red cedar, pine branches with small cones (Virginia pine is used here, but use what is available to you), waxmyrtle branches, grapevine coiled into a wreath (about 18 to 20 inches here), Spanish moss
- Nativar: *Juniper virginiana* 'Grey Owl'
- Garden-grown: Arizona cypress 'Silver Star'
- Extra goodies: peacock feathers, pheasant feathers, turkey feathers—whichever suits your fancy

## ASSEMBLY

First, you'll need a sturdy frame. A hand-wrapped grapevine one like this works beautifully. Just don't use one of those box store versions—they are too thick and heavy, and you will be loading this up enough as it is. If grapevine isn't handy, use a double-ring metal version like the one shown in the Rabbit Tobacco Wreath demo.

Also, find a nice large work surface, like the 4-by-8-foot surface featured here, and put a trash/compost can just below or beside the table—things will get messy.

**1.** Start by laying out an evergreen base in piles of one to three stems, depending on their thickness, in several even-numbered rows. Juniper 'Grey Owl,' with its nearly teal-shaded foliage, is used here, but any type of evergreen pine, fir, cypress, or cedar is fine. Avoid deciduous hardwoods because the wood isn't flexible—and flexible is best for the base. How many piles? Rule of thumb: wreath frame diameter (in inches) equals number of piles needed. It the diameter is an odd number, round up for shorter greenery and down for longer.

**2.** Next, lay down berried cedar on every other pile. It is advantageous to organize the rows and piles so the alternating materials line straight up the rows on the table.

**3.** A long piece of Arizona cypress is added to every other pile that doesn't have cedar on it. Now you can see what I mean about layout. It will come in handy soon.

**4.** Magnolia is next! Rule of thumb: magnolia stem count equals half of wreath diameter inches. Strip most of the lower leaves from the stem until six or so remain. Hold each stem vertically and see which way the terminal leaves unfold and recall an actual magnolia flower—their orientation depends on where it was growing on the tree. The ultimate continuity of the wreath begins here: foliage "flowers" that turn left, others that go right, and full facing stems are placed alternately on every other pile of cedar. Work from the top right corner, go left, drop down to the next row or start at the bottom. When assembling the wreath, start in one corner and add piles, moving horizontally across the row. Pull from the next row just below the beginning of the previous. (Visualize eating corn on the cob or an old-school typewriter—just hit "return"!)

**5.** Gently arched branches of pine are laid on the silver cypress piles. Again, consider the natural direction they curve and try to alternate the placement. Waxmyrtle branches were added to the magnolia alternately as the supply allowed. If they are available, add plenty because their silver berries really do stand out!

**6.** Using a roll of florist wire, begin to wrap the piles onto the frame. Notice that the silver cypress is situated on the right side of the frame and the pine toward the center left. Never begin with a magnolia bunch. The wood is brittle and lifting that first bundle up in order to cram in the final material may result in an unfortunate "snap" sound. (If that does happen, simply wire in the broken pieces at the end of wrapping.)

**7.** Magnolia bunch #1 goes in. Lay it down on the other greens so that it opens like a flower. Strip any excess lower leaves that get in the way of the wire wrap.

**8.** The next pile of greens goes in, sliding the feature greens under the previous magnolia leaves on each side. This time, the pine is placed on the outside of the frame and the silver cypress heads toward the center. Alternating these very different looking materials each time adds balance and allows them to dance around the circle without being obvious circles themselves. If you add berries or any other standout material, do the same.

**9.** Another magnolia bunch is added to the frame and the open flower placement continues. This branch has an obvious crook to its stem, and it is situated accordingly. The other option would be to cut it at that 90-degree bend and tuck the branch deeper down in the base, keeping that foliage open and flowering.

**10.** Continue working around the frame until about three-quarters of it has been filled. Step back, take stock, and consider the last quarter of bunches needed. If fewer bunches are needed than the original estimate, plan their placement so that the final bunch is still one with magnolia in it.

**11.** This is what the wreath should look like before the final bunch with magnolia is added.

**12.** The last bunch is added and secured, and the wire is looped and finished as shown in previous demos. The last bunch of materials always needs an extra twist of adjustment. Once hung, add flourishes to make it your own, like a bit of Spanish moss set to hang as it naturally does from our coastal plain trees.

# A Gilded Fascinator

When I first started making gilded magnolia wreaths many years ago, I was inspired by the gold, silver, copper, and bronze tones that the evergreens I was using took on in the winter. A light coating of spray paint on the big leaves of the magnolia seemed a perfect counter to the naturally metallic greens of various cypress, cedar, and spruce needles. Even Fraser fir branches, when turned upside down, have a silvery white cast to them. After that, I started thinking about the highly decorative gilded frames that surround fine works of art and high-end mirrors. I thought it would be fun to reverse the practice of art imitating nature and create natural frames that imitate those skillfully crafted works of art in a dramatic way. The sculptural shapes of my favorite materials are highly accented when they are shined up, and they also last a very long time.

## MATERIALS

**Note:** When you are getting everything together, make sure to have several long pieces (3-plus feet) of evergreen and sago palm.

- Natives: magnolia, pine branches, pinecones, saw palmetto, eastern red cedar, smilax, beech branches, waxmyrtle
- Non-natives: Arizona cypress 'Carolina Sapphire' and 'Silver Star,' sago palm, jimson weed pods

## ASSEMBLY

First of all, a sturdy frame is needed. Using a bolt cutter, I cut two diagonal corners of a 20-inch square clamp frame to get the corner shape I needed. Another option would be adding several corner screws to hold a couple of

20-by-2-inch boards together to get the same shape. Nails can be hammered in along both sides of each length at 3- to 4-inch intervals, mimicking the clamps on the metal frame and creating stable anchors for the wrapping wire that holds everything in place. You will, of course, also need metallic paint suitable for floral crafts. A good selection (as pictured here) can be found at most hobby stores or can be ordered from a floral supply company. *Do not* use spray paint that is meant for covering up rust from the hardware store—it doesn't work.

**1.** Gather the plant materials you want to use together on a big table and, besides the already metallic evergreens, decide which varieties get what metal coating. Aside from the magnolia and smilax, I assign one color to each variety: white pine—14K Gold, Virginia pine—Super Silver, sago palm—Brilliant Silver, saw palmetto—Brilliant Gold. For the magnolia, I did four each of 24K Gold, Copper, and Brilliant Silver. For the smilax, two very long pieces are Super Silver, and multiple short pieces are 14K Gold.

Holding a *dry* stem upright, give it a *light* coating of paint, making sure you get the front and back of the pines. If stems are wet or the paint is laid on too thickly, it will peel off at the slightest touch. Allow the paint to dry before you begin laying it all out.

**2.** Beginning with those that will extend across and down the door frame, lay out piles. Those first two, shown here on the far left with the silver sago in them, need to be long, with long pieces of evergreen as the base. The longest one will go down the side of the door or window, while the one going across the top will be proportionately shorter. The next three sets of piles should be laid out to mirror one another.

**3.** Secure two rolls of wire to the frame, one on each end. This makes it so much easier to continually work each side. It is also fine to wrap each pile to one side first and then do the other if that is easier. It's up to you.

**4.** Consider which way the final product will be mounted on the door—either the left corner or the right corner—and place the first long piles accordingly. There are five clamps on each side of the frame, and for stability, seat each pile in between the first two of those clamps. Wrap the wire tightly from the end toward the corner; you don't want the top piece to schlump from its own weight from not being anchored properly when it is hung.

**5.** The second set of piles is set into the third clamp on each side and wrapped tightly. If needed, tuck any materials that overlap the previous magnolia pieces behind them, so they don't get lost.

**6.** Continuing to work toward the corner, add the next set of piles into the fourth clamp on each side and secure.

**7.** When you reach the corner with the last set of piles, the tips of each will overlap. When you are placing them, adjust the materials if needed so that they come together at pleasing angles. Once both are secured with the wire, cut the wire of one roll and anchor the end to the frame so it doesn't come undone—you only need one now.

**8.** Time to soften the corner with some additional handfuls of greenery. A bunch of white pine is placed with the tips pointing diagonally inward and secured with the wire.

**9.** A handful of coppery magnolia foliage and silvery waxmyrtle is laid to point diagonally up and out from the corner to fill the void that naturally happens. More gilded pine is added to the back of this bunch to fluff it up even more. **Note:** If it had been readily available, I would have used lots more waxmyrtle in this design!

**10.** This is what it looks like now that the corner has been filled in. It still needs to be finished, and the following steps are an easy way to do so.

**11.** Select five pinecones that are roughly the same size and a sixth that is slightly smaller. Lay them out in a star pattern.

**12.** Using the roll of wire you removed from the frame in Step 7, wrap it around the base of the first pinecone as pictured, getting it down in the core of the cone. Leave some length on the wire's end—you will need it before too long.

**13.** Attach each pinecone by wrapping the wire around the core of each at the base with the wire and continuing to the next until you've finished the fifth. Attach the fifth cone to the first cone to complete the star. Twist the wire ends together and cut the roll.

**14.** Lay the open star on the open corner of the fascinator piece and anchor down securely with wire.

**15.** Place the sixth, smaller pinecone on the center of the star and anchor it down using the same method of wire wrapping used to make the star. Cut the wire.

**16.** Prepare to hang your pretty work! Hammer several long nails (with a wide head) across the top of the door frame. Make sure they are in deep enough to hold the weight of the piece. Hang the fascinator. Once it is in place, it can be secured further by carefully running wire around its base and then twisting the wire around the nails.

**17.** Time to fluff! I tucked in beech branches, more magnolia, and jimson weed pods to give the piece more texture and movement. I also wired more pine to the tail because it needed to be longer. You could even make your creation pool at the ground if you wanted to—just be careful to place the materials so that they don't interfere with the inevitable comings and goings that happen around doors.

# Azulejos Wreath

Azulejos are the tiles made in Portugal, and the colors of this wreath recall that. The circle is our world, blues are the water, green plants keep us breathing, and the yellow sun makes it all happen. The gilded smilax is because we are all attracted to shiny things—gold to be specific. Short gray days beg for light, and the progression of this design is a good demonstration of my quest for brightness. I started with just the blue berries, some juniper, and the gilded vines, but everything kept falling flat when I put it together. Out of frustration, I grabbed some round, yellow horse nettle fruits, and the sun came out. Sometimes, composing a successful design can be an exercise in trial and error, and I am sharing that insight with you in this process.

## TOOLS

Gloves with leather palms, Design Master craft spray (I used the 14K Gold), cheap gold-colored craft wire, metal rickrack wreath frame or a thin, home-made grapevine one (I used a 20-inch frame, but it can easily be scaled up or down)

## MATERIALS

- Smilax, some with blue berries and many without
- Eastern red cedar (*Juniperis virginiana*)
- Mountain laurel, pine, American holly (select stressed branches that have become more yellowed)
- Fruited horse nettle stems: This is a native perennial that isn't covered in the plant guide because it is not something you want to fool with any

other time of year because the tiny thorns are evil. That said, once winter rolls around and the clusters of persistent yellow fruits shine and the thorns have softened with the rest of the stems, they become hard to resist—and you need to be wearing gloves anyway for this design.

## ASSEMBLY

**1.** Lightly coat both the smilax stems that do not have berries and the wreath frame on both sides with craft spray. I am also using matching wire because this is a more openly formed wreath and I wanted whatever shows to look good with the smilax.

**2.** Composing a visually striking design is often an exercise in trial and error. After initially laying out my piles of smilax stems, wrapping them on a smaller 12-inch frame, and adding the cedar, I was displeased with the effect. In search of a visual "pop," I laid out different bits and pieces I had on hand and found the solution in tones of warm gold and olive.

**3.** I tweaked the overall color effect a bit more with the addition of Virginia pine branches. I love finding pine along roadsides that is yellowed from the lack of nutrition.

**4.** The new palette is laid out and a bigger frame is chosen.

**5.** Lay the pine around the frame. If there is a finite amount of a particular material, it's always a good idea to plan in advance on how you want it distributed.

**6.** Lay other key ingredients out around the frame so you know how the voids will be filled.

**7.** Lay out the alternating "piles" so that they will be ready for you to grab as you work around the wreath. Because the gilded smilax vine can be rather tangly, keep it and the cedar to the side and add them as you go.

**8.** Although I typically point the tips of my materials to the right and wrap so the frame moves counter-clockwise as I go, I chose to work in the opposite direction on this one because the pine's growth habit looked better if I situated it that way. Make the most of your material's natural beauty.

**9.** Continue working around the frame, adding the cedar and smilax in even doses. Longer pieces of the cedar look good flopping out a bit, not only balancing the pine but also bringing movement to the piece.

**10.** Almost there! If it looks like you are running short on materials at this point, stop and scrounge around for more or start spacing the piles slightly farther apart.

**11.** Step back and check your work. This looks cool just the way it is and could be finished now for a different look.

**12.** Otherwise, time to cram in that last bunch of materials and finish off the wire as shown in the previous wreath demonstrations.

**13.** When it comes to fresh wreaths, the finished product will hang better if it is allowed to lay flat in a cool, dry spot for two to four days. This allows the materials to cure and the long pieces to set so they don't flop in funny ways if they are at the top of the form.

# GLOSSARY OF TERMS

**Alternate leaves:** Alternate leaves and buds are situated along a stem alternately and not directly across from each other.

**Annual:** An annual is a plant that completes its growth cycle within one growing season. Annuals sprout from seeds and grow into a mature plant, flower, produce seeds, and then die within a matter of months.

**Biennial:** A biennial is a plant that usually completes its growth cycle within two growing seasons. Biennials will often germinate and produce only low-growing foliage the first season, then after a cold, dormant period will send up flowering stalks, produce seeds, and die in the second growing season.

**Bract:** A bract is a specialized leaf that often surrounds true flowers (the actual reproductive parts). The white "petals" of a flowering dogwood are not petals but actually bracts. Another example of a bract is the green "cup" surrounding the stem of flame honeysuckle just below its cluster of flowers.

**Chlorosis/Chlorotic:** Chlorosis describes the lightened discoloration of foliage —either partial or whole—due to nutritional deficiencies. Chlorotic leaves display a lighter color across the entire surface, between the veins, or only along the veins as compared to their healthy counterparts. Examples: If there is a nitrogen deficiency in a plant, the entire surface of its lower leaves will become chlorotic and show as yellow. A magnesium deficiency causes interveinal chlorosis, which means that while there is yellowing in the area between, the veins remain green.

**Compound leaf:** Compound leaves are structures that emerge from a stem with more than one leaf situated on its petiole. The petiole is the part of a leaf that attaches it to the stem. A bud is located on the stem in the axil of the petiole.

**Cultivar:** Plant cultivars are names given outside of the actual genus and species when they are selected or bred for distinguishing features differing from their parents and then propagated. A cultivar name follows the genus and species with single quotation marks around it.

**Dioecious-Dicot:** Plant species that are individually either male or female, but not both.

**Dormant:** A plant is considered dormant when its herbaceous growth is not actively growing. Although a perennial or tree may be dormant from the ground up, the roots and all of the living mycorrhizal communities that are associated with those roots are still active below the surface of the soil.

**DOT, or Department of Transportation:** County, state, or federal departments that are responsible for road and road right-of-way ownership and maintenance.

**Drupe:** A drupe is a berry-like fruit whose colored skin surrounds a fleshy layer with a harder inner layer that surrounds a single seed. Holly berries are drupes.

**Fauna:** The largest kingdom of living organisms, encompasses animals of any kind, including insects, but not plants. The counterpart of flora.

**Flora:** This kingdom of multicellular organisms, including algae, make their own food through photosynthesis. They are not animals and not fungi. The counterpart of fauna.

**Floret:** A single flower within a closely arranged cluster of flowers on a single flower stalk or bract.

**Foliage:** The leafy green, chlorophyll-producing part of a vascular plant.

**Fungi:** Fungi are a kingdom consisting of multicellular organisms that do not produce their own food. They are neither flora nor fauna. Some species of fungi have evolved complex, beneficial relationships with flora, while other species have evolved to prey on or exploit flora and fauna resources to the detriment of those species.

**Genus:** The biological classification ranking between family and species, consisting of structurally or phylogenetically related species or a single isolated species exhibiting unusual differentiation (monotypic genus). The genus name is the first word of a binomial scientific name (the species name being the second word).

**Inflorescence:** An inflorescence is a group of flowers growing from a common stem, often in a characteristic arrangement.

**Leaflet:** Anywhere between three to hundreds of individual leaflets make up a compound leaf.

**Monecious-Monocot:** Plant species whose individuals have both male and female flowering parts.

**Mycorrhiza:** Beneficial mycorrhiza are the vascular-type filaments of a network of fungi that grow with the roots of a plant, forming a symbiotic relationship with those roots.

**Nativar:** A relatively new term coined to describe a cultivar of a native plant species.

**Node:** A plant node is the point along the stem from which buds, flowers, and leaves emerge.

**Opposite leaves:** Opposite leaves and associated buds emerge from a stem directly across from one another in a mirrored fashion.

**Perennial:** A perennial plant is one that, after it has reached maturity, completes a vegetative and reproductive growth period within a season, dies back to the ground, entering a dormant period, and then repeats the whole process again the following year. Short-lived perennials, like columbine species, may go through this process for three years before they give up (although these types usually leave plenty of offspring in the general vicinity). On the other end of the spectrum, long-lived perennials, such as *Baptisia* species, set deep taproots and may thrive for decades.

**Pistil:** The pistil is the female part of a flower that catches the pollen and ultimately produces a seed or seeds.

**Raceme:** A raceme is the shape of a cluster of flowers that emerge at even intervals from one long stem, with the lowest ones opening first.

**Rhizome:** Rhizomes are fleshy, rootlike stems that creep horizontally underground and send up perennial shoots of growth from nodes. Solomon's seal grows from a rhizome.

**Samara:** A dry fruit or seed capsule with wings to carry it through the breeze. Maple trees have samara that spin like helicopters when they fall.

**Scape:** A scape is a non-woody stalk without leaves or nodes that emerges between basal leaf growth and culminates in a flower. Onions and daylilies produce scapes.

**Serrated:** A leaf is described as serrated when the edges look like the cutting edge of a saw.

**Species:** In scientific terms, a plant's species name comes after the genus name. Plant species are a group that share common physical characteristics and can freely breed with one another and produce offspring that share the same characteristics.

**Stamen:** The stamen is the male, pollen-producing part of a flower.

**Stoloniferous:** Used to describe the growth habit of a plant that spreads.

**Sucker:** A plant sucker is a vigorous shoot of growth that emerges from the root system away from the main stem, or around the base of a trunk if the plant is in distress. If a hardwood tree is chopped down, suckers can be observed the following growth season surrounding the girth of the original trunk.

**Tendril:** A tendril is a threadlike, specialized leaf on a vine that is used for climbing other plants or structures. Their mode of action varies from one species to the next: Some have a tiny claw or claws at the tip, allowing the tendril to cling to whatever surface it touches; others have cells along one side of the tendril that contract when they are touched, causing the tendril to curl around the available support it reaches; while other tendrils have tips with sticky pads, allowing them to stick to whatever support they touch.

**Umbel:** An umbel is an inflorescence characterized by a rounded, upward-facing, flat top consisting of many small individual florets that originate from a common point. Think of an opened umbrella. Golden alexanders and carrot flowers have umbel-shaped flowers.

**Vine:** A vine is a plant that sometimes creeps but usually climbs other plants and structures using specialized stems, leaves, and thorns.

**Whorled leaf:** A whorled leaf is one that emerges from a stem with two or more other leaves and their buds at the same node. Imagine looking straight down at a spinning top.

**Woody plant:** Woody plants are trees, shrubs, and vines that produce hard, woody tissue.

# BIBLIOGRAPHY

**PIEDMONT REGION DESCRIPTION**

Piedmont Summary. USGS. sciencebase.gov/catalog/item /55c77fc4e4b08400b1fd8350.

Rummer, R. B.; Hafer, M. L. 2014. *Outlook for Piedmont Forests: A Sub-Regional Report from the Southern Forest Futures Project.* Gen. Tech. Rep. SRS-195. Asheville, NC: US Department of Agriculture Forest Service, Southern Research Station.

**LONGLEAF PINE STATISTICS**

"America's Forgotten Forest." National Wildlife Federation. nwf.org /Magazines/National-Wildlife/2008/Americas-Forgotten-Forest.

Longleaf Pine Ecosystem. Wikipedia. en.wikipedia.org/wiki/Longleaf _pine_ecosystem.

NC Longleaf Coalition. nclongleaf.org/llPineForests.html.

**SPECIES RANGE MAPS**

Sarracenia Groves, M., ed. 1993. *Horticulture, Trade and Conservation of the Genus Sarracenia in the Southeastern States of America: Proceedings of a Meeting Held at the Atlanta Botanical Garden, September 22–23, 1993.*

USDA, NRCS. 2019. The PLANTS Database (http://plants.usda.gov, 15 July 2019). National Plant Data Team, Greensboro, NC 27401-4901 USA.

Vine etymology. merriam-webster.com/dictionary/vine.

## BOOKS

Armitage, Allan M., and Judy M. Laushman. *Specialty Cut Flowers: The Production of Annuals, Perennials, Bulbs and Woody Plants for Fresh and Dried Cut Flowers, 2nd Edition*. Portland, OR: Timber Press, 2003.

Bell, C. Ritchie, and Bryan J. Taylor. *Florida Wild Flowers and Roadside Plants*. Chapel Hill, NC: Laurel Hill Press, 1982.

Dirr, Michael A. *Manual of Woody Landscape Plants: Their Identification, Ornamental Characteristics, Culture, Propagation and Uses, 4th Edition*. Champaign, IL: Stipes Publishing LLC, 1990.

Dole, John, and Lane Greer. *Woody Cut Stems for Growers and Florists: Production and Post-Harvest Handling of Branches for Flowers, Fruit, and Foliage*. Portland, OR: Timber Press, 2009.

Hinkley, Dan J. *The Explorer's Garden: Rare and Unusual Perennials*. Portland, OR: Timber Press, 1999.

——. *The Explorer's Garden: Shrubs and Vines from the Four Corners of the World*. Portland, OR: Timber Press, 2009.

Ingham, Vicki L. *Elegance in Flowers: Classic Arrangements for All Seasons*. Birmingham, AL: Oxmoor House, 1985.

Justice, William S., and C. Ritchie Bell. *Wild Flowers of North Carolina*. Chapel Hill: University of North Carolina Press, 1987.

Kasperski, Victoria R. *How to Make Cut Flowers Last*. New York, NY: Gramercy Publishing Company, 1957.

Nelson, Gil. *East Gulf Coastal Plain Wildflowers: A Field Guide to the Wildflowers of the East Gulf Coastal Plain, Including Southwest Georgia, Northwest Florida.* Guilford, CT: FalconGuides, 2005.

# INDEX

bowl gardens, miniature, 145–49
Bowman's root (*Gillenia trifoliata*), 4, 44–45
bride's feathers (*Aruncus dioicus*), 25–26
Brownie Points (design), 159–61
brown recluse spider, 7, 8
bubby bush (*Calycanthus floridus*), 99–100
butterfly milkweed (*Asclepias tuberosa*),
  29, 170
Butterfly Milkweed Mix (design), 170–72

caffeine, 112
*Callicarpa americana* (beautyberry), 98–99,
  208, 212, 216
*Callicarpa dichotoma* (purple beautyberry),
  98
*Calycanthus floridus* (Carolina allspice,
  sweet shrub, bubby bush), 99–100
*Campsis radicans* (trumpet vine), 81,
  170, 183
Carolina allspice (*Calycanthus floridus*),
  99–100
Carolina jessamine (*Gelsimium sempervirens*), 84, 151
Carolina lily (*Lilium michauxii*), 50–51
*Cercis canadensis* (eastern redbud), 100–101
Chartreuse and Purple (design), 208–11
chicory (*Cichorium intybus*), xvi
*Chionanthus virginicus* (fringetree, greybeard), 101–2, 157
chocolate, 80, 159, 216
city foraging, 5–6
*Clematis terniflora* (sweet autumn
  clematis), 82
*Clematis virginiana* (virgin's bower,
  traveler's joy), 3, 82–83, 205
clothing, 7–8, 11
Coastal Plain Abundance (design), 156–58
Columbian era, xiii
columbine (*Aquilegia canadensis*), 24, 151
common milkweed (*Asclepias syriaca*), 28
*Conoclinium coelestinum* (blue mistflower,
  ageratum), 34, 192, 208
copperhead snake, 8
coralberry (*Symphoricarpos orbiculatus*),
  138–39, 225
*Coreopsis lanceolata* (lanceleaf tickseed), 35
*Coreopsis nudata* (Georgia tickseed), 35
*Coreopsis* sp., 35–36, 201, 208, 216
*Coreopsis verticillata* (whorled tickseed), 35

*Cornus alternifolia* (pagoda dogwood, alternate leaf dogwood), 102–3, 163
*Cornus ammomum* (silky dogwood), 104
*Cornus florida* (flowering dogwood), 105
*Cornus* sp. (dogwood), 102–5, 151, 153
*Corylus americana* (wild hazelnut, American
  filbert), 106, 195
*Cotinus* 'Purple Smoke,' 45
cottonmouth snake, 8
crabapple (*Malus angustifolia*), 123
*Crateagus* (hawthorn), 9
creeping fig (*Ficus pumila*), 77, 87
crossvine (*Bignonia capreolata*), 80
cucumber tree (*Magnolia fraseri*), 120,
  122–23
cultivar names, defined, xv–xvi
Curtis' goldenrod (*Solidago curtisii*), 68

dame's rocket (*Hesperis matronalis*), 75
*Daucus carota* (Queen Anne's lace), xvi, 180
deer resistant, 70
devil's darning needles (*Clematis virginiana*), 82
devil's hair (*Clematis virginiana*), 82
devil's walking stick (*Aralia spinosa*), 97–98
dewberry (*Rubus flagellaris*), 134, 135–36
*Dioscorea villosa* (wild yam vine), 83–84
*Diospyros virginiana* (persimmon), 107
Dirr, Michael, 110–11, 114
dog fennel (*Eupatorium capillifolium*), 36–37
dogwood (*Cornus* sp.), 102–5, 151, 153
Dooly, Vince, 111
downy phlox (*Phlox pillosa*), 53, 188, 192

eastern coral snake, 8
eastern hemlock (*Tsuga canadensis*), xiii–xiv
eastern redbud (*Cercis canadensis*), 100–101
eastern red cedar (*Juniperus virginiana*),
  116–17, 225, 228–33, 234, 241
elderberry (*Sambucus canadensis*), 136–37
English ivy (*Hedera helix*), 6, 77, 87
*Epifagus virginiana* (beech drops), 108
eupatorium, 4
*Eupatorium capillifolium* (dog fennel),
  36–37
*Eupatorium fistulosum* (Joe pye weed),
  39–40
*Eupatorium maculatum* (Joe pye weed),
  39–40

*Ilex decidua* (winterberry, possomhaw), 113, 113–14
*Ilex glabra* (gallberry, inkberry), 112, 113–14
*Ilex opaca* (American holly), 113–14, 241
*Ilex* sp. (holly), 85, 111–14, 167, 241
*Ilex vomitoria* (yaupon holly), 85, 112, 113–14
*Illicium floridanum* (Florida anise), 114–15
*Illicium floridanum* 'Florida Sunshine,' 115
*Illicium floridanum* 'Halley's Comet', 114–15
*Illicium parviflorum* (yellow anisetree), 115
Indian current (coralberry, *Symphoricarpos orbiculatus*), 138–39, 225
Indian-physic (*Gillenia trifoliata*), 4, 44–45
inkberry (*Ilex glabra*), 112, 113–14
insects, 6–7
introduced (naturalized) species, xvi
invasive species, xvi–xviii
ironweed (*Vernonia*), 72–74
*Itea virginica* 'Saturn,' 116
*Itea virginica* (Virginia sweetspire), 115–16, 157

Jackson vine (*Similax smallii*), 90–91
jack vine (*Aristolochia macrophylla*), 79
Joe pye weed (*E. fistulosum, E. maculatum, E. purpureum*), 39–40
*Juniperus virginiana* 'Brodie,' 116–17
*Juniperus virginiana* (eastern red cedar), 116–17, 225, 228–33, 234, 241

*Kalmia latifolia* (mountain laurel), 4, 118–19, 241
kudzu, xvii

lanceleaf tickseed (*Coreopsis lanceolata*), 35
Late Autumn Spectrum (design), 216–18
Lavender and Peach (design), 188–91
*Lepidium virginicum* (pennycress, pepper grass), 48–49, 174
*Liatris* sp. (gayfeather, blazing star), 49–50, 188, 208, 216, 219
*Lilium michauxii* (Carolina lily), 50–51
*Lilium superbum* (Turk's cap lily), 50–51, 183
*Liriodendron tulipifera* (tulip poplar), 119–20, 163
*Lobelia amoema* (southern lobelia), 51
*Lobelia siphilitica* (blue lobelia, fan flower), 51–52, 192

longleaf pine (*Pinus palustris*), xiv–xv
*Lonicera sempervirens* (flame honeysuckle, trumpet honeysuckle), xv, 85, 151
Lunar New Year (design), 153–55
*Lupinus perennis* (sundial lupine), 52–53
lyre leaf sage (*Salvia lyrata*), 65–66

Magnolia and Cedar Wreath (design), 228–33
*Magnolia fraseri* (cucumber tree), 120, 122–23
*Magnolia grandiflora* (southern magnolia), 121, 122–23
*Magnolia* sp., xiv, 120–23, 183, 228–33, 234
*Magnolia virginiana* (sweetbay magnolia), 121–23
*Maianthemum racemosum* (false Solomon's seal, Solomon's plume), 53–54, 163, 195
*Malus angustifolia* (southern crabapple), 123
maple (*Acer* sp.), 95–97, 216
Maypop Blue and Cool Pink in a Compote (design), 192–94
maypop (*Passiflora incarnata*), 89, 192
*Mentha* (mint), xvi
milkweed (*Asclepias* sp.), 3, 16, 26–29, 170
Miniature Bowl Gardens (design), 145–49
mint (*Mentha*), xvi
mock orange (*Philadelphus inodorus*), 45, 100, 126–27, 159
*Monarda didyma* 'Raspberry Wine,' xv–xvi
*Monarda didyma* (scarlet bee balm), xv–xvi, 51
*Monarda fistulosa* (wild bergamot), 188
*Monarda* sp. (bee balm), xv–xvi, 4, 51, 54–55, 188, 195
moss phlox (*Phlox subulata*), 58–59, 146, 156
mountain decumbent goldenrod (*Solidago curtisii*), 68
mountain laurel (*Kalmia latifolia*), 118–19, 241
mountain mint (*Pycnanthemum* sp.), 62–63, 183, 188
muscadine (grapevine, *Vitis*), 91, 174, 229
*Myrica cerifera* (waxmyrtle), 4, 124–25, 219, 229, 234

nativars, xvi
native plants, overview
    definition and descriptions, xv

# ABOUT THE AUTHOR

LEE HEMMINGS CARLTON is a horticulturist, flower farmer, and garden designer who is seldom without a pair of clippers. Since her days at the University of Georgia learning from the great plantsmen, Dr. Michael A. Dirr and Dr. Allan Armitage, she's worked designing, growing for, installing, and maintaining large private gardens in Georgia, the Carolinas, and Florida. Through Lee's cut flower and landscape business—Goldenrod Gardens—flowers, fruits, and foliage are sustainably foraged or grown to supply local florists for weddings, workshops, and everyday designs. She is also a florist in her own right and has made thousands of bouquets, flowered plenty of weddings and large events, and made  hundreds of natural wreaths throughout her career. Her primary flower crop is dahlias selected or bred by her specifically for floral design. Originally a native of Moultrie, Georgia, she now resides in the mountains of North Carolina—west of Boone and Banner Elk—with her husband, David Wimmer. When not busy with the nature of plants, she can be found taking pictures of them, traveling the Southeast, or swimming just about anywhere.